TEACHER'S PET PUBLICATIONS

LITPLAN TEACHER PACK
for
Anne Frank: The Diary of a Young Girl
based on the dairy by
Anne Frank

Written by
Mary B. Collins

© 1999 Teacher's Pet Publications
All Rights Reserved

This **LitPlan** for
Anne Frank: Diary of a Young Girl
has been brought to you by Teacher's Pet Publications, Inc.

Copyright Teacher's Pet Publications 1999
11504 Hammock Point
Berlin MD 21811

Only the student materials in this unit plan
such as worksheets, study questions, assignment sheets, and tests
may be reproduced multiple times for use in the purchaser's classroom.

For any additional copyright questions,
contact Teacher's Pet Publications.

www.tpet.com

TABLE OF CONTENTS - *Anne Frank: Diary of a Young Girl*

Introduction	5
Unit Objectives	8
Reading Assignment Sheet	9
Unit Outline	10
Study Questions (Short Answer)	13
Quiz/Study Questions (Multiple Choice)	21
Pre-reading Vocabulary Worksheets	31
Lesson One (Introductory Lesson)	47
Nonfiction Assignment Sheet	49
Oral Reading Evaluation Form	54
Writing Assignment 1	48
Writing Assignment 2	52
Writing Assignment 3	70
Writing Evaluation Form	71
Vocabulary Review Activities	63
Extra Writing Assignments/Discussion ?s	61
Unit Review Activities	72
Unit Tests	75
Unit Resource Materials	105
Vocabulary Resource Materials	119

*Note: Normally we would include biographical information about the author on the next page(s), but since this work is autobiographical, there seems to be little point in including the usual "About the Author" page(s).

INTRODUCTION

This unit has been designed to develop students' reading, writing, thinking, and language skills through exercises and activities related to *Anne Frank: Diary of a Young Girl* by Anne Frank. It includes eighteen lessons, supported by extra resource materials.

The **introductory lesson** introduces students to background information about places, people and events Anne Frank mentions in her diary. It also doubles as the first writing assignment for the unit. Following the introductory activity, students are given a transition to explain how the activity relates to the diary they are about to read. Following the transition, students are given the materials they will be using during the unit.

The **reading assignments** are approximately thirty pages each; some are a little shorter while others are a little longer. Students have approximately 15 minutes of pre-reading work to do prior to each reading assignment. This pre-reading work involves reviewing the study questions for the assignment and doing some vocabulary work for 8 to 10 vocabulary words they will encounter in their reading.

The **study guide questions** are fact-based questions; students can find the answers to these questions right in the text. These questions come in two formats: short answer or multiple choice. The best use of these materials is probably to use the short answer version of the questions as study guides for students (since answers will be more complete), and to use the multiple choice version for occasional quizzes. If your school has the appropriate equipment, it might be a good idea to make transparencies of your answer keys for the overhead projector.

The **vocabulary work** is intended to enrich students' vocabularies as well as to aid in the students' understanding of the diary. Prior to each reading assignment, students will complete a two-part worksheet for approximately 8 to 10 vocabulary words in the upcoming reading assignment. Part I focuses on students' use of general knowledge and contextual clues by giving the sentence in which the word appears in the text. Students are then to write down what they think the words mean based on the words' usage. Part II nails down the definitions of the words by giving students dictionary definitions of the words and having students match the words to the correct definitions based on the words' contextual usage. Students should then have an understanding of the words when they meet them in the text.

After each reading assignment, students will go back and formulate answers for the study guide questions. Discussion of these questions serves as a **review** of the most important events and ideas presented in the reading assignments.

After students complete reading the work, a lesson is devoted to the **extra discussion questions/writing assignments**. These questions focus on interpretation, critical analysis and personal response, employing a variety of thinking skills and adding to the students' understanding of the diary.

Following the discussion there is a **vocabulary review** lesson which pulls together all of the fragmented vocabulary lists for the reading assignments and gives students a review of all of the words they have studied.

The **group activity** has students working in small groups to discuss the diary as a portrait of war, a philosophy of life, a portrait of adolescence, or a study in the nature of people. Using the information they have acquired so far through individual work and class discussions, students get together to further examine the text and to brainstorm ideas relating the diary to one of these topics.

The group activity is followed by a **reports and discussion** session in which the groups share their ideas about the topics with the entire class; thus, the entire class is exposed to information about each topic, and the entire class can discuss each topic based on the nucleus of information brought forth by each of the groups.

There are three **writing assignments** in this unit, each with the purpose of informing, persuading, or having students express personal opinions. The first assignment is to inform: students write a composition about one of the background topics assigned in Lesson One. The second assignment is to express personal opinions: students will keep a diary for the duration of the unit. The third assignment is to persuade: students pretend to be Anne, and try to convince Mummy to alter her treatment of Anne to the way Anne would like to be treated.

The **nonfiction reading assignment** is tied in with Writing Assignment 1 and the introductory lesson. Students are required to read a piece of nonfiction related in some way to *Anne Frank: Diary of a Young Girl*. In this case, the topics are assigned in Lesson One. After reading their nonfiction pieces, students will fill out a worksheet on which they answer questions regarding facts, interpretation, criticism, and personal opinions. During one class period, students make **oral presentations** about the nonfiction pieces they have read. This not only exposes all students to a wealth of information, it also gives students the opportunity to practice **public speaking**.

The **review lesson** pulls together all of the aspects of the unit. The teacher is given four or five choices of activities or games to use which all serve the same basic function of reviewing all of the information presented in the unit.

The **unit test** comes in two formats: multiple choice or short answer. As a convenience, two different tests for each format have been included. There is also an advanced short answer unit test for higher level students.

There are additional **support materials** included with this unit. The **extra activities** section includes suggestions for an in-class library, crossword and word search puzzles related to the diary, and extra vocabulary worksheets. There is a list of **bulletin board ideas** which gives the teacher suggestions for bulletin boards to go along with this unit. In addition, there is a list of **extra class activities** the teacher could choose from to enhance the unit or as a substitution for an exercise the teacher might feel is inappropriate for his/her class. **Answer keys** are located directly after the **reproducible student materials** throughout the unit. The student materials may be reproduced for use in the teacher's classroom without infringement of copyrights. No other portion of this unit may be reproduced without the written consent of Teacher's Pet Publications, Inc.

UNIT OBJECTIVES *Anne Frank: Diary of a Young Girl*

1. Students will study Anne Frank's *Anne Frank: Diary of a Young Girl* as a portrait of war, a portrait of adolescence, a philosophy of life, and a study of the nature of people.

2. Students will demonstrate their understanding of the text on four levels: factual, interpretive, critical, and personal.

3. Students will do background research to make the diary more meaningful.

4. Students will discuss specific passages from the diary to deepen their understanding of the people and ideas presented by Anne Frank.

5. Students will discuss ways one can 'make do' with what one has--to stretch a budget, create nutritious meals from staples, etc.

6. Students will be given the opportunity to practice reading aloud and silently to improve their skills in each area.

7. Students will answer questions to demonstrate their knowledge and understanding of the main events and characters in Anne Frank: Diary of a Young Girl as they relate to the author's theme development.

8. Students will enrich their vocabularies and improve their understanding of the diary through the vocabulary lessons prepared for use in conjunction with the diary.

9. The writing assignments in this unit are geared to several purposes:
    a. To have students demonstrate their abilities to inform, to persuade, or to express their own personal ideas
        Note: Students will demonstrate ability to write effectively to <u>inform</u> by developing and organizing facts to convey information. Students will demonstrate the ability to write effectively to <u>persuade</u> by selecting and organizing relevant information, establishing an argumentative purpose, and by designing an appropriate strategy for an identified audience. Students will demonstrate the ability to write effectively to <u>express personal ideas</u> by selecting a form and its appropriate elements.
    b. To check the students' reading comprehension
    c. To make students think about the ideas presented by the diary
    d. To encourage logical thinking
    e. To provide an opportunity to practice good grammar and improve students' use of the English language.

READING ASSIGNMENT SHEET - *Anne Frank*

Date Assigned	RA#	Sections to be Read	Completion Date
	1	6/14/42 - 9/29/42	
	2	10/1/42 - 2/27/43	
	3	3/10/43 - 8/10/43	
	4	8/18/43 - 1/6/44	
	5	1/7/44 - 2/28/44	
	6	3/1/44 - 3/31/44	
	7	4/1/44 - 8/1/44	

UNIT OUTLINE - *Anne Frank: Diary of a Young Girl*

1 Library Writing Assignment #1	2 Introduction	3 PVR 1	4 PVR 2	5 Study ?s 1&2 PVR 3 Assign VR 4
6 Speaker	7 Group Activity	8 VR 5	9 VR 6	10 "Potato Day" Assign VR 7
11 Study ?s 3-7 Extra ?s	12 Vocabulary	13 Quotations	14 Group Activity	15 Reports & Discussion Diaries Due
16 Writing Conference Writing Assignment 3	17 Review	18 Test		

Key: P = Preview Study Questions   V = Prereading Vocabulary Worksheet   R = Read   RA = Reading Assignment

STUDY GUIDE QUESTIONS

SHORT ANSWER STUDY GUIDE QUESTIONS - *Anne Frank: Diary of a Young Girl*

June 14, 1942 - February 27, 1943

1. Who was Anne Frank?
2. Identify and give a brief description of:
   Margot Frank -
   Otto Frank -
   Mrs. Frank -
3. The Franks' ability to prepare the "hidden house" and survive living there for two years would have been impossible were it not for a group of protectors. Identify Mr. Kraler, Mr. Koophuis, Meip, and Elli.
4. When does Anne's diary begin? Why is this day special?
5. What is meant by the saying, "Paper is more patient than man"?
6. Give a brief sketch of Anne's life prior to the beginning of the diary.
7. What were some of the restrictions placed on the Dutch Jews by the Germans?
8. What forces the Franks into hiding?
9. Where is the secret annexe located?
10. On July 13th, the Van Daan family arrives. Identify and briefly describe Mr. Van Daan, Mrs. Van Daan and Peter Van Daan.
11. What contact do the Franks and Van Daans have with the outside world?
12. In September, Peter and Anne begin their studies, usually under the direction of Mr. Frank. What do they study?
13. Because of their close confinement and constant association with each other, friction among them occurs frequently. What are some of the clashes?
14. What is the big news from the outside world in November of 1942?
15. In November another person comes to live in the secret annexe. Describe this newcomer.
16. What was Mr. Van Daan's previous occupation? How does he make use of it now?
17. What special event brightens the Christmas holidays?
18. Are conditions better as the year 1943 begins?
19. In February, Mr. Frank thinks the invasion may be soon. Is he correct?

Anne Frank: Diary of a Young Girl Short Answer Study Guide Page 2

March 1, 1943 - August 1, 1944

1. On May 1, 1943, Anne's entry takes stock of their situation. Has it improved?
2. As their first year in hiding draws to a close, two more disasters strike. Describe them. (June 15th entry)
3. July of 1943 brings Anne and her fifty-four year old roommate into a confrontation. What was the source of this row?
4. How is the war progressing in the summer of 1943?
5. The daily routine of life in the annexe grinds on. The days are monotonous and seem to stretch on to infinity. How does this affect Anne and the others?
6. In the Netherlands, St. Nichols Day is the traditional day to exchange gifts. Last year there was a basket of presents. What do they do this year to celebrate?
7. What do the "family" members receive at Christmas from their protectors?
8. Anne ends her third six months in hiding with an awakening maturity. What evidence of this growth is reported in her diary?
9. Has life in the Annexe changed much as the last six months begin?
10. All during the spring Anne's entries in her diary are mainly about her personal life: her first kiss, her reflections on the frictions in the group. In March there is an exchange of letters. Who are the two correspondents? What does the exchange accomplish?
11. Although Anne is not much interested in politics, one entry in March of 1944 tells about the various opinions of the group. what are the prevailing viewpoints?
12. What has happened to the morale of some Dutch citizens?
13. The breakdown of a sense of right and wrong brings on the greatest fright the family has had to date. Describe what happened.
14. What momentous event occurred in June of 1944?
15. The diary ends on August 1, 1944. What happens to Anne and her "family"?

ANSWER KEY: SHORT ANSWER STUDY GUIDE QUESTIONS
Anne Frank: Diary of a Young Girl

June 14, 1942 - February 27, 1943

1. Who was Anne Frank?

    Anne Frank was a young girl, born June 12, 1929 to an upper-middle class Jewish family. Her father, Otto Frank, saw the danger to the Jews long before Hitler had his "final solution" for all Jews in place. When Anne was four years old, in 1933, the family moved to Holland where her father had business connections.

2. Identify and give a brief description of:

    Margot Frank - Margot was Anne's beautiful, intelligent sister who was three years older than Anne. She is often held up as a model of what Anne should try to become.

    Otto Frank - Mr. Frank is Anne's father. He is several years older than Anne's mother. He is intelligent and well-educated. Mr. Frank usually plays the role of peacemaker in the frequent bickering that take place in their confined quarters.

    Mrs. Frank - "Mummy" is eleven years younger that Mr. Frank. She has been used to having servants in the house to do the work. Consequently, when the responsibility for cleaning and cooking falls mainly upon her shoulders, she is often incompetent and rather disorganized.

3. The Franks' ability to prepare the "hidden house" and survive living there for two years would have been impossible were it not for a group of protectors. Identify Mr. Kraler, Mr. Koophuis, Meip, and Elli.

    Mr. Kraler - When Jews were no longer allowed to own a business, he assumed management of those which Mr. Frank and Mr. Van Daan had run. He helped them prepare the "Secret Annexe" and later provided material supplies as well as psychological support. All of this involved extreme risk to himself, even though he was not a Jew.

    Mr. Koophuis - He, along with Mr. Kraler, takes over the running of the business. Like Kraler, he too is a Dutch Gentile. He is especially helpful in arranging the logistics of obtaining food.

    Meip - Meip is a young woman who works in the office of the business. She too helps to secure food and is particularly good at raising the spirits of those in the annexe. Her husband's name is Henk.

    Elli - Elli is another young office worker who helps with collecting food. Like Meip, she also helps keep spirits up.

4. When does Anne's diary begin? Why is this day special?

    It begins on June 14, 1942, Anne's birthday.

5. What is meant by the saying, "Paper is more patient than man"?
    See June 20, 1942 entry. People may weary of listening to adolescent "unbosomings," but a piece of paper just patiently receives whatever the writer wishes to write on it.

6. Give a brief sketch of Anne's life prior to the beginning of the diary.
    Anne was born in Frankfort, Germany. The family migrated to Holland in 1933 when Anne's father became a partner in Kolen and Co.

7. What were some of the restrictions placed on the Dutch Jews by the Germans?
    They had to wear the yellow star and to hand in their bicycles. They were banned from trains and forbidden to drive. They could only shop between three and five o'clock and then only at "Jewish" shops. They had to be indoors by eight o'clock P.M. All sports and sports facilities were forbidden. They could not visit Christians, and they had to attend Jewish schools.

8. What forces the Franks into hiding?
    In early July, Margot, who was sixteen, received a "call up notice" which meant she would be deported to a concentration camp. It was unthinkable that Margot should go. The only alternative was to hide and try to survive.

9. Where is the secret annexe located?
    It is in the same building where Mr. Frank's office and warehouse were located. There is a hidden entrance behind a cupboard. Part of the second floor and all of the third floor which was not bare attic, made up their living quarters. The building itself is located in downtown Amsterdam.

10. On July 13th, the Van Daan family arrives. Identify and briefly describe Mr. Van Daan, Mrs. Van Daan and Peter Van Daan.
    Mr. Van Daan is a business associate of Mr. Frank.
    Mrs. Van Daan is an interesting, opinionated woman. In the beginning Anne finds her very difficult to get along with. Later she finds her to be a good listener and talks to her more than she does her own mother.
    Peter Van Daan is two and a half years older than Anne. His quiet personality is a great contrast to Anne's chatterbox tendencies.

11. What contact do the Franks and Van Daans have with the outside world?
    In the office there is a secret radio where broadcasts from England can be heard. Although Anne and the others fear to listen, the desire to know what is going on prevails and they tune in almost every day. News from nearby is brought to them by their protectors.

12. In September, Peter and Anne begin their studies, usually under the direction of Mr. Frank. What do they study?

    Anne studies French. Peter struggles with English. Anne works with her father on his family tree. Later (October) Elli writes for a correspondence course in shorthand for them. Anne has trouble with math, but she loves to read. Her passion is mythology.

13. Because of their close confinement and constant association with each other, friction among them occurs frequently. What are some of the clashes?

    Mr. and Mrs. Van Daan "yell" at each other. Mrs. Van Daan is annoyed by Anne's chatter and shirks her dishwashing duties when it is her turn. Anne's mother and Mrs. Van Daan frequently tangle, which seems to be based on a simple personality conflict. Peter is moody and a hypochondriac. Anne had believed that only children squabbled, but now she believes that adults can be as petulant as children. Anne, the youngest, eems to be the most frequent scapegoat. She says you can only really get to know people when you've had a "jolly good row with them."

14. What is the big news from the outside world in November of 1942?

    The Allied forces invaded Africa and there is news of victories.

15. In November another person comes to live in the secret annexe. Describe this newcomer.

    Mr. Dussel is an elderly dentist who must share Anne's room. Margot will sleep on the camp bed. Anne finds him slow on the uptake. He brings sad news of many of their friends who have been deported. It is hard to remain cheerful in the face of this enormous brutality. Mr. Dussel turns out to be a "sermonizer" and lectures Anne very often about her "manners." Worse than that, he runs to Mummy, who lectures her all over again.

16. What was Mr. Van Daan's previous occupation? How does he make use of it now?

    Mr. Van Daan used to be in the meat, sausage and spice business and now makes sausages in order to preserve some black market meat for future use in case times "get harder."

17. What special event brightens the Christmas holidays?

    Each person will receive an extra 1/4 pound of butter, which they decide they will use to make biscuits and cakes to celebrate.

18. Are conditions better as the year 1943 begins?

    No; indeed, they are much worse. More and more Jews are being dragged away. Dutch young men are sent to the front. "Everyone is afraid." To add to this, air raids continue night after night. Dutch children go about without warm clothing from cold house to cold street to cold classrooms. Countless children beg a piece of bread from strangers in the street. Amidst all of this misery, nerves snap and Anne is reminded daily of her faults, a situation she does not enjoy. No wonder there are frequent blow-ups.

19. In February, Mr. Frank thinks the invasion may be soon. Is he correct?
    No, the invasion is a long way off. The winter months are not a suitable time for an all-out invasion. Perhaps he says this to lighten their despair. The food is in short supply and not very good. The attic is full of rats, and Peter is bitten. The tedium is almost unbearable. To make matters worse, there is some evidence that thieves are snooping about the warehouse.

March 1, 1943 - August 1, 1944

1. On May 1, 1943, Anne's entry takes stock of their situation. Has it improved?
    About the only thing that has gotten better is the weather. Their food is inadequate and verges on being inedible. Breakfast is dry bread and ersatz coffee. Dinner is spinach or lettuce and small potatoes that are nearly rotten. Their clothes are frayed, none too clean, and way to small in Anne's case, as well as Margot's.

2. As their first year in hiding draws to a close, two more disasters strike. Describe them. (June 15 entry)
    Elli's father, Mr. Vassen, has cancer which is too far along to respond to surgery. "He was our best helper and security advisor." The second blow is that they must turn in their big radio. It has been their "source of courage" and it is doubtful if a small set can bring in overseas' broadcasts.

3. July of 1943 brings Anne and her fifty-four year old roommate into a confrontation. What was the source of this row?
    Anne wishes to use a writing table in her room for one and one half hours, two afternoons a week. Mr. Dussel, up until now, has been using it full-time. Mr. Dussel is in the secret annexe as a guest. One might think he would be loath to claim anything but his bed for his exclusive use. It is indicative, however, of Anne's low status, that he feels she has no rights at all, and until Anne's father takes a hand, he refuses to allow Anne to spend any time at all at the writing table.

4. How is the war progressing in the summer of 1943?
    The air raids are increasing, sometimes as many as two a day. The happiest war news is that Mussolini has "resigned" and the Fascist party has been outlawed in Italy.

5. The daily routine of life in the annexe grinds on. The days are monotonous and seem to stretch on to infinity. How does this affect Anne and the others?
    Worry and depression assail all of them. They have "almost forgotten how to laugh." They fear the approaching winter. Will there be any heat? Will there be enough food when provisions from the gardens are no longer available? By October Anne reports everybody is ready to abuse almost anyone. Anne, and of course, all the others, live in constant fear. In November, Mr. Dussel has been with them one year. He marks the occasion by giving Mrs. Frank a plant, but he speaks not one word of gratitude to anyone.

6. In the Netherlands, St. Nichols Day is the traditional day to exchange gifts. Last year there was a basket of presents. What do they do this year to celebrate?

    Anne and her father compose a little poem for each person and place them in the owners' shoes. All shoes are placed in a decorated basket. Hopes are not very high this year. "The war is at a standstill. Morale rotten."

7. What do the "family" members receive at Christmas from their protectors?

    Meip has made a cake with "Peace 1944" written on it. Elli has supplied a pound of cookies (sweet biscuits of pre-war quality). The young people each receive a bottle of yogurt, and the elders are provided with a bottle of beer each.

8. Anne ends her third six months in hiding with an awakening maturity. What evidence of this growth is reported in her diary?

    She re-evaluates her evaluation of her mother and is startled to read her scathing remarks in the preceding year. Her interest in her own body's development quickens, and her interest in the opposite sex begins to bloom. She shows a new appreciation of all their protectors have done for them.

9. Has life in the Annexe changed much as the last six months begin?

    No. The daily routine is not any different. The war news is more optimistic, and everyone awaits the invasion which they know must come. Anne's inner life, however, is much changed. She still resents being cooped up and being treated like a child who should be seen and not heard, but now she can share her thoughts with Peter, who shares his feelings with her.

10. All during the spring Anne's entries in her diary are mainly about her personal life: her first kiss, her reflections on the frictions in the group. In March there is an exchange of letters. Who are the two correspondents? What does the exchange accomplish?

    Anne and Margot exchange letters and the result is a better understanding between them. Anne has been feeling guilty about her budding romance with Peter because she thought Margot cared for him. Margot answers her that she cares for him only as a younger brother.

11. Although Anne is not much interested in politics, one entry in March of 1944 tells about the various opinions of the group. what are the prevailing viewpoints?

    They seem to divide basically into two groups: the optimists who say the war is going well and who have great faith in the English, and the pessimists who believe the Germans will win in the end. All seem to admire Winston Churchill; all agree the Germans lie about many things and that on the whole the B.B.C. does not lie.

12. What has happened to the morale of some Dutch citizens?
    They are hungry and cold most of the time. Their clothes are in rags. Looting and thieving are quite common. This is not true of the majority who provided food coupons for those in hiding and turned a blind eye to may happenings which led them to surmise that people were in hiding in the secret annexe.

13. The breakdown of a sense of right and wrong brings on the greatest fright the family has had to date. Describe what happened.
    On Easter Sunday, burglars again entered the warehouse. Although the burglars are dangerous to them, the police are a greater danger. If someone reports the break in, police will search the whole place and the family will be discovered. In a later entry we learn that a green grocer who lived nearby did discover the broken board, but he decided not to report it to the police. The man said, "I don't know anything but I guess a lot." He is just one example of how the Dutch tried to protect those in hiding.

14. What momentous event occurred in June of 1944?
    The invasion of Europe began on the French peninsula and seemed to be succeeding. The family is ecstatic and listens to the radio more than ever. Anne's fifteenth birthday is celebrated with more joy than usual.

15. The diary ends on August 1, 1944. What happens to Anne and her "family"?
    They are rounded up by the Gestapo who probably acted on information from an informer. Anne died in Bergen Belsen. The only survivor in the group was Mr. Frank.

MULTIPLE CHOICE STUDY GUIDE/QUIZ QUESTIONS
Anne Frank: Diary of a Young Girl

June 14, 1942-February 27, 1943

1. Who was Anne Frank?
    A. She was a British girl who grew up in India during the time that India was fighting for independence from Great Britain.
    B. She was an American girl who migrated to the West with one of the first wagon trains.
    C. She was a white girl living in South Africa who thought apartheid was wrong and fought for black equality.
    D. She was an upper middle-class Jewish girl who lived in Holland during the time of the Holocaust.

2. Match the character and the description.
    1. Margot Frank   A. sometimes disorganized and incompetent
    2. Otto Frank   B. enthusiastic and talkative
    3. Mrs. Frank   C. quiet, beautiful, and intelligent
    4. Anne Frank   D. well educated; often the peacemaker

3. Match the characters and the descriptions.
    1. Mr. Kraler   A. particularly good at keeping spirits up
    2. Mr. Koophuis   B. helped prepare the "Secret Annexe"
    3. Meip   C. also helps with collecting food
    4. Elli   D. takes over running Mr. Frank's business

4. When does Anne's diary begin? Why is this day special?
    A. It begins on June 14, 1942, Anne's birthday.
    B. It begins on September 8, 1941, Anne's first day of high school.
    C. It begins on December 19, 1942, the first day of Hanukkah.
    D. It begins on February 21, 1941, the day of Anne's first date.

5. Refer to the June 20, 1942 entry. What is meant by the saying, "Paper is more patient than man"?
    A. A piece of paper can exist longer than a person.
    B. People may make written promises, but they don't always keep them.
    C. People may weary of listening to adolescent chatter, but a piece of paper patiently receives whatever the writer puts on it.
    D. A secret is better kept if it is written on paper than if it is told to another.

Anne Frank: The Diary of a Young Girl Multiple Choice Study Questions Page 2

6. Which describes Anne's life prior to the beginning of the diary?
    A. She was born in London and moved to New Delhi when she was three. Her father was a colonel in the British Army.
    B. She was born in Frankfort, Germany. She moved to Holland when her father went into business there.
    C. She was born in New York. Her father wanted to become a landowner, and moved the family to Oregon on a wagon train.
    D. She was born in Paris. Her father was a political activist, and moved the family to South Africa so he could work for civil rights for the Blacks.

7. Which was not a restriction placed on the Dutch Jews by the Germans?
    A. wearing a yellow star on all clothes
    B. not riding their bicycles or driving
    C. only speaking Hebrew
    D. shopping between three and five o'clock in the afternoon

8. What forces the Franks into hiding?
    A. Margot receives a notice that she is to be deported to a concentration camp.
    B. The family does not have enough money to flee to America.
    C. Mr. Frank is suspected of visiting Christians.
    D. A neighbor is making up stories about them disobeying the restrictions.

9. Where is the secret annexe located?
    A. It is in the country, in a barn on Meip's father's farm.
    B. It is in downtown Amsterdam, in the building where Mr. Frank's office and warehouse were located.
    C. It is just outside the city, in an orphanage.
    D. It is in the city, in the church Mr. Kraler attends.

10. Match the characters and the descriptions.
    1. Mr. Van Daan   A. good listener, interesting and opinionated
    2. Mrs. Van Daan   B. quiet, not too friendly at first
    3. Peter Van Daan   C. business associate

11. What contact do the Franks and Van Daans have with the outside world?
    A. They don't have any contact, because it is much too dangerous.
    B. They get the newspaper every day from Mr. Koophuis.
    C. They listen to a radio in the office, and hear from their protectors.
    D. They receive occasional letters from friends who have managed to hide in other areas.

Anne Frank: The Diary of a Young Girl Multiple Choice Study Questions Page 3

12. In September Peter and Anne begin their studies under the direction of Mr. Frank. What do they study?
    A. They both study Hebrew and world history.
    B. Anne studies literature, and Peter studies science.
    C. Anne studies French, and Peter studies English.
    D. They both study math and Latin.

13. Which is not one of the clashes they have because of their confinement?
    A. Mr. and Mrs. Van Daan yell at each other.
    B. Anne and Margot vie for Peter's attention.
    C. Mrs. Van Daan shirks her dishwashing duties.
    D. Anne's chatter annoys the others.

14. What is the big news from the outside world in November of 1942?
    A. The Allied Forces invade Africa and there is news of victories.
    B. The Japanese bomb Pearl Harbor and the United States retaliates.
    C. The Germans are taking over Paris.
    D. The Russians are opposing the Germans.

15. Describe Mr. Dussel and what life is like after he comes to live in the secret annexe.
    A. He is young and cheerful. He Anne, Margot, and Peter begin to have lively discussions and things don't seem so bad.
    B. He is self-centered and monopolizes the attention of Mrs. Frank and Mrs. Van Daan. The children are irritated and feel ignored.
    C. He is a middle aged man who has traveled around the world. He entertains them with stories of his travels.
    D. He is an elderly dentist who brings sad news of their friends. He lectures Anne and complains about her to her mother.

16. What was Mr. Van Daan's previous occupation? How does he make use of it now?
    A. He was an engineer for an Amsterdam radio station. He is able to tune in their radio and repair it when it breaks.
    B. He was a college professor. He is able to advance the children in their studies.
    C. He was in the meat, sausage, and spice business. He makes sausages to preserve some black market meat.
    D. He was a rabbi. He is able to help the others keep their courage by telling them stories from the Old Testament.

Anne Frank: The Diary of a Young Girl Multiple Choice Study Questions Page 4

17. What special event brightens the Christmas holidays?
    A. There is a Christmas tree in the warehouse. They can sneak down to look at it at night.
    B. Each person receives an extra 1/4 pound of butter, which they use to make biscuits and cakes.
    C. They are able to sneak out for a walk around the warehouse.
    D. Meip brings new clothes for Anne, Peter, and Margot.

18. Describe conditions as the year 1943 begins.
    A. Things are much better. The Allies are progressing. There is more food. Restrictions on the Jews are easing.
    B. Things are much worse. More Jews are being dragged away. People are cold and hungry. There are nightly air raids.
    C. Things are about the same. There is little heat, but a little more food. The Gestapo are not as intent at removing Jews.
    D. Things are terrible. The Dutch have agreed to turn in all of the Jews who are in hiding.

19. Which of these does not describe conditions in February?
    A. Food is in short supply.
    B. Peter is bitten by a rat.
    C. Amsterdam is inundated by a blizzard and no one can move.
    D. Thieves are snooping around in the warehouse.

Anne Frank: The Diary of a Young Girl Multiple Choice Study Questions Page 5

<u>March 1, 1943-August 1, 1944</u>

20. Which does not describe the situation in Anne's entry of May 1, 1943?
    A. The winter has been unusually long and harsh.
    B. The food is inadequate and almost inedible.
    C. The clothes are frayed and dirty.
    D. Anne and Margot are outgrowing their clothes.

21. Refer to the June 15 entry. What two disasters strike?
    A. The plumbing breaks and can't be fixed. Peter becomes very ill, but can't risk going to a doctor.
    B. Meip is ill and can't bring food for a week. It becomes dangerous to have any lights on, and they must stay in the dark at night.
    C. Mr. Vassen has inoperable cancer. They must turn in the big radio.
    D. Mr. Frank runs out of money. They find out that their home and possessions have all been destroyed.

22. July of 1943 brings Anne and Mr. Dussel into a confrontation. What is it about?
    A. Anne wants to stay up late reading and Mr. Dussel wants to go to sleep early.
    B. Anne wants to bring Peter's cat into their room. Mr. Dussel does not want her to, because he says he is allergic to it.
    C. Anne and Margot want to spend one night together and have Mr. Dussel sleep in the front room. He refuses to do it.
    D. Anne wishes to use a writing table in her room on two afternoons a week. Mr. Dussel is using it full time and does not want to share.

23. How is the war progressing in the summer of 1943?
    A. The Germans are weakening in some areas, although not in Holland. There is hope that it will be over soon.
    B. There are more air raids. Mussolini has resigned and the Fascist party has been outlawed in Italy.
    C. It is going badly for the Allies. The heat is slowing them down.
    D. It looks like the war may be over any day. Hitler cannot withstand the pressure from the Allies.

Anne Frank: The Diary of a Young Girl Multiple Choice Study Questions Page 6

24. How is daily life in the secret annexe affecting the group?
    A. They are worried and depressed, and are beginning to abuse one another.
    B. They are fearful, yet still optimistic.
    C. They have become very close to one another. The arguments have ceased, and there is a tranquility about the place.
    D. They hate one another and are so tired of living in the secret annexe that they talk of turning themselves in.

25. What do they do to celebrate St. Nichols Day?
    A. They each do two good deeds for one of the others.
    B. Mr. Dussel shares a bottle of wine that he had saved.
    C. Anne and her father write a poem for each person.
    D. They sing traditional songs and tell stories of the old days.

26. What do the "family" members receive at Christmas from their protectors?
    A. Meat, potatoes, and apples
    B. Sweet biscuits, yogurt, and beer
    C. Cigarettes and a new radio
    D. New blankets and pillows

27. Anne ends her third six months in hiding with an awakening maturity. Which is not a sign of her growth?
    A. She has started to write a novel.
    B. She realizes she has been cruel to her mother.
    C. She is becoming interested in the opposite sex.
    D. She shows a new appreciation for their protectors.

28. How has life for Anne changed as the last six months begin?
    A. She can no longer tolerate Mr. Dussel and has moved to the front room.
    B. She and her mother are on good terms, but Margot is jealous.
    C. The others are tired of her noise and refuse to speak to her.
    D. She can now share her thoughts with Peter.

Anne Frank: The Diary of a Young Girl Multiple Choice Study Questions Page 7

29. In March there is an exchange of letters. Who are the two correspondents? What does the exchange accomplish?
    A. The letters are between Mr. Frank and Mr. Kraler. Mr. Frank is able to start making arrangements in case they are freed soon.
    B. They are between Mr. and Mrs. Van Daan. They agree to write instead of yelling, and everyone is relieved.
    C. They are between Peter and Mr. Dussel. They realize they have a lot in common, and Mr. Dussel becomes more pleasant.
    D. They are between Anne and Margot. They develop a better understanding of their respective feelings about Peter.

30. One entry in March of 1944 refers to politics. On what do all of the members of the group agree?
    A. They all admire Winston Churchill.
    B. They all think the war is going well.
    C. They all think the B.B.C. tells lies.
    D. They all think the Germans will win.

31. What has happened to the morale of some Dutch citizens?
    A. They are tired of Hitler and secretly plan a rebellion.
    B. They begin looting and thieving.
    C. They think they will be better off if they turn in all of the Jews.
    D. They join Hitler out of desperation.

32. What happens on Easter Sunday?
    A. Anne and Peter share their first kiss.
    B. The protectors bring a feast.
    C. The police follow Meip and she can't come to see the group.
    D. Thieves break in to the warehouse again.

33. What event occurred in June of 1944?
    A. The invasion of Europe began.
    B. Anne and Peter announced their engagement.
    C. Mr. Frank escaped safely from the secret annexe.
    D. A group of soldiers moved into the warehouse.

34. The diary ends on August 1, 1944. What happens to Anne and the others?
    A. They are rounded up by the Gestapo. All die except Mr. Frank.
    B. They leave the secret annexe. The Franks and Peter escape, but the others are caught.
    C. The protectors smuggle them all to safety in the country.
    D. They all commit suicide rather than surrender to the Germans.

ANSWER KEY - MULTIPLE CHOICE STUDY/QUIZ QUESTIONS
Anne Frank: Diary of a Young Girl

June 14, 1942-February 27, 1943
1. D.
2. 1, C; 2, D; 3, A; 4, B.
3. 1, B; 2, D; 3, A; 4, C.
4. A.
5. C.
6. B.
7. C.
8. A.
9. B.
10. 1, C; 2, A; 3, B.
11. C.
12. C.
13. B.
14. A.
15. D.
16. C.
17. B.
18. B.
19. C.

March 1, 1943 - August 1, 1944
20. A.
21. C.
22. D.
23. B.
24. A.
25. C.
26. B.
27. A.
28. D.
29. C.
30. A.
31. B.
32. D.
33. A.
34. A.

PREREADING VOCABULRY WORKSHEETS

VOCABULARY - *Anne Frank: Diary of a Young Girl*

<u>6/14/42 - 9/29/42</u> Part I: Using Prior Knowledge and Contextual Clues

Below are the sentences in which the vocabulary words appear in the text. Read the sentence. Use any clues you can find in the sentence combined with your prior knowledge, and write what you think the underlined words mean in the space provided.

1. I take little notice of <u>ardent</u> looks and pedal blithely on.

2. I am by no means a <u>fanatic</u>, but I have a leaning that way and find it interesting.

3. Daddy has been at home a lot lately, as there is nothing for him to do at business; it must be rotten to feel so <u>superfluous</u>.

4. For months as many of our goods and <u>chattels</u> and necessities of life as possible had been sent away . . . .

5. Also, she is thoroughly <u>piqued</u> that her dinner service and not ours is in use.

6. Sour faces and <u>obstinate</u> silences for three days and then everything went smoothly once more.

7. I am not such a <u>prude</u> that I can't talk about these things.

Anne Frank Vocabulary Worksheet 6/14/42 - 9/29/42 Continued

Part II: Determining the Meaning: Match the vocabulary words to their dictionary definitions.

___ 1. ardent
___ 2. fanatic
___ 3. superfluous
___ 4. chattels
___ 5. piqued
___ 6. obstinate
___ 7. prude

A. Stubborn
B. Personal, movable property
C. One who is excessively concerned with being proper
D. Fervent; passionate
E. Person with an extreme enthusiasm for something
F. Provoked; full of resentment
G. Not needed

Vocabulary - *Anne Frank: Diary of a Young Girl* 10/1/42 - 2/27/43

Part I: Using Prior Knowledge and Contextual Clues

Below are the sentences in which the vocabulary words appear in the text. Read the sentence. Use any clues you can find in the sentence combined with your prior knowledge, and write what you think the underlined words mean in the space provided.

1. She said that I was quite attractive and that I had nice eyes. Rather vague, don't you think?

2. Is it just a chance that Daddy and Mummy never rebuke Margot and that they always drop on me for everything?

3. I can't always be drawing attention to her untidiness, her sarcasm, and her lack of sweetness, neither can I believe that I'm always in the wrong.

4. He is known to be quiet, and . . . both families think he is a congenial person.

5. But Dussel was immediately plied with questions from all sides.

6. We pass the time in all sorts of crazy ways . . . . But it all begins to pall in the end.

7. . . . keep my thoughts to myself, and try for *once* to be just as disdainful to them as they are to me.

8. I have procured another little notebook for foreign words.

Anne Frank Vocabulary Worksheet 10/1/42 - 2/27/43 Continued

Part II: Determining the Meaning: Match the vocabulary words to their dictionary definitions.

__ 8. vague   A. Friendly
__ 9. rebuke   B. To become dull or boring
__ 10. sarcasm   C. Reprimand; criticize
__ 11. congenial   D. Despicable; contemptible
__ 12. plied   E. Not clearly expressed; inexplicit
__ 13. pall   F. To get by special effort; obtain
__ 14. disdainful   G. Cutting remarks
__ 15. procured   H. Assailed

Vocabulary - *Anne Frank: Diary of a Young Girl* 3/10/43 - 8/10/43

Part I: Using Prior Knowledge and Contextual Clues

Below are the sentences in which the vocabulary words appear in the text. Read the sentence. Use any clues you can find in the sentence combined with your prior knowledge, and write what you think the underlined words mean in the space provided.

1. . . . the burglars disappeared and the only sounds that Mr. Van Daan could hear were the heartbeats of the frightened <u>fatalist</u> herself.

2. For myself, I remain silent and <u>aloof</u>, and I shall not shrink from the truth any longer . . . .

3. It will be our turn to hand in our radio next month. Koophuis has a <u>clandestine</u> baby set at home that he will let us have to take the place of our big Phillips.

4. I get on better by <u>shamming</u> a bit, instead of my old habit of telling everyone exactly what I think.

5. You are already <u>proficient</u> in the theory, it's only the practice that you lack.

6. First, I hear a sound like a fish gasping for breath, this is repeated nine or ten times, then with much <u>ado</u> and interchanged with little smacking sounds, the lips are moistened . . . .

7. The former is the most <u>unassuming</u> of all at table. He looks first to see if everyone else has something. He needs nothing himself, for the best things are for the children.

Anne Frank Vocabulary Worksheet 3/10/43 - 8/10/43 Continued

Part II: Determining the Meaning
    You have tried to figure out the meanings of the vocabulary words for 3/10/43 - 8/10/43. Now match the vocabulary words to their dictionary definitions. If there are words for which you cannot figure out the definition by contextual clues and by process of elimination, look them up in a dictionary.

___ 16. fatalist
___ 17. aloof
___ 18. clandestine
___ 19. shamming
___ 20. proficient
___ 21. ado
___ 22. unassuming

A. Bustle; fuss; bother
B. Modest
C. Reserved; remote
D. Adept; expert
E. One who believes all events are predetermined and inevitable
F. Kept secret to conceal an improper purpose
G. Putting on a false appearance

Vocabulary - *Anne Frank: Diary of a Young Girl* 8/18/43 - 1/6/44

Part I: Using Prior Knowledge and Contextual Clues
   Below are the sentences in which the vocabulary words appear in the text. Read the sentence. Use any clues you can find in the sentence combined with your prior knowledge, and write what you think the underlined words mean in the space provided.

1. Mr. Dussel begins, does not always scrape well, but scrapes <u>incessantly</u>, glancing right and left.

2. . . . the wonderful news of Italy's <u>capitulation</u> came in.

3. The atmosphere is so <u>oppressive</u>, and sleepy and as heavy as lead.

4. And when I asked him . . . whether I should congratulate or <u>condole</u>, he answered that it didn't matter to him.

5. He has become very <u>tolerant</u>.

6. I imagine a mother as a woman who, in the first place shows great <u>tact</u>, especially towards her children when they reach our age, and who does not laugh at me if I cry about something-- not pain, but other things--like "Mums" does.

7. One thing, which perhaps may seem rather <u>fatuous</u>, I have never forgiven her.

Anne Frank Vocabulary Worksheet 8/18/43 - 1/6/44 Continued

Part II: Determining the Meaning: Match the vocabulary words to their dictionary definitions.

___ 23. incessantly
___ 24. capitulation
___ 25. oppressive
___ 26. condole
___ 27. tolerant
___ 28. tact
___ 29. fatuous

A. To express sympathy
B. Inclined to put up with beliefs, practices or traits of others
C. Foolish
D. Continually, without interruption
E. Ability to act or speak without offending
F. Difficult to bear; weighing heavily on the senses or spirit
G. Surrender under specified conditions

Vocabulary - *Anne Frank: Diary of a Young Girl* 1/7/44 - 2/28/44

Part I: Using Prior Knowledge and Contextual Clues

Below are the sentences in which the vocabulary words appear in the text. Read the sentence. Use any clues you can find in the sentence combined with your prior knowledge, and write what you think the underlined words mean in the space provided.

1. I love you, and with such a great love that it can't grow in my heart any more but has to leap out into the open and suddenly <u>manifest</u> itself in such a devastating way!

2. . . . we can sympathize with the sufferings of people who get taken away, and rejoice with the <u>liberated</u> prisoner.

3. On Sunday evening everyone except Pim and me was sitting beside the wireless in order to listen to the "<u>Immortal</u> Music of the German Masters."

4. This gave me rather a pang; it seems such a pity that there's always just a <u>tinge</u> of dishonesty about him.

5. She looks at me so <u>queerly</u> every time I go into Peter's little room.

6. Oh, who knows, perhaps it won't be long before I can share this overwhelming feeling of <u>bliss</u> with someone who feels the way I do about it.

7. Like you, I long for freedom and fresh air, but I believe now that we have ample <u>compensation</u> for our <u>privations</u>.

8. I hide my feelings, throw my weight about the place, am noisy and <u>boisterous</u>, so that everyone wishes that I was out of the way.

Anne Frank Vocabulary Worksheet 1/7/44 - 2/28/44 Continued

Part II: Determining the Meaning: Match the vocabulary words to their dictionary definitions.

___ 30. manifest   A. Freed
___ 31. liberated   B. Oddly
___ 32. immortal   C. Lack of basic necessities of life
___ 33. tinge   D. Loud; lacking in restraint or discipline
___ 34. queerly   E. Show plainly; reveal
___ 35. bliss   F. Slight addition
___ 36. compensation   G. Never to be forgotten
___ 37. privations   H. Offset; counterbalance; repayment
___ 38. boisterous   I. Extreme happiness

Vocabulary - *Anne Frank: Diary of a Young Girl* 3/1/44 - 3/31/44

Part I: Using Prior Knowledge and Contextual Clues
    Below are the sentences in which the vocabulary words appear in the text. Read the sentence. Use any clues you can find in the sentence combined with your prior knowledge, and write what you think the underlined words mean in the space provided.

1. I finally managed to ask him today whether he didn't find my chatter a <u>nuisance</u>; he only said: "It's okay, I like it!"

2. I can tell by Peter's face that he thinks just as much as I do, and when Mrs. Van Daan yesterday evening said <u>scoffingly</u>: "The thinker!" I was irritated.

3. That's all I was--a terrible flirt, <u>coquettish</u> and amusing.

4. I would never have dreamed of cribbing from anyone else. I shared my sweets generously, and I wasn't <u>conceited</u>.

5. I couldn't understand it, I was taken by surprise, and the only way I could keep up some bearing was by being <u>impertinent</u>.

6. . . . I know I am not prejudiced, I don't exaggerate so much, I am more precise and <u>adroit</u> and because of this--you may laugh--I feel superior to her in a great many things.

Part II: Determining the Meaning: Match the vocabulary words to their dictionary definitions.

___ 39. nuisance   A. Characteristic of a woman who makes teasing romantic overtures
___ 40. scoffingly   B. Skillful & adept under pressure
___ 41. coquettish   C. Bother
___ 42. conceited   D. Characterized by holding an unusually high opinion of oneself
___ 43. impertinent   E. Mockingly
___ 44. adroit   F. Improperly forward or bold

Vocabulary - *Anne Frank: Diary of a Young Girl* 4/1/44 - 8/1/44

Part I: Using Prior Knowledge and Contextual Clues
　　Below are the sentences in which the vocabulary words appear in the text. Read the sentence. Use any clues you can find in the sentence combined with your prior knowledge, and write what you think the underlined words mean in the space provided.

1. The men were <u>perplexed</u> at such impudence . . . .

2. I want to send in to some paper or other to see if they will take one of my stories, under a <u>pseudonym</u>, of course.

3. In my diary I treat all the privations as amusing. . . . and that is the <u>sole</u> reason why I have to laugh at the humorous side of the most dangerous moments.

4. A great <u>din</u> and disturbance followed, and Mouschi, who had finished by that time, dashed downstairs.

5. I don't think I shall easily bow down before the blows that <u>inevitably</u> come to everyone.

6. I <u>loathe</u> having to tell you this, but why shouldn't I, if I know it's true anyway?

Part II: Determining the Meaning: Match the vocabulary words to their dictionary definitions.

___ 45. perplexed　　　A. Only
___ 46. pseudonym　　B. Hate; extreme dislike
___ 47. sole　　　　　　C. Troubled with uncertainty
___ 48. din　　　　　　 D. Unavoidably
___ 49. inevitably　　　E. A fictitious name used by an author
___ 50. loathe　　　　　F. Hate; extremely dislike

ANSWER KEY - VOCABULARY
Anne Frank: Diary of a Young Girl

6/14/42 - 9/29/42
1. D
2. E
3. G
4. B
5. F
6. A
7. C

10/1/42 - 2/27/43
8. E
9. C
10. G
11. A
12. H
13. B
14. D
15. F

3/10/43 - 8/10/43
16. E
17. C
18. F
19. G
20. D
21. A
22. B

8/18/43 - 1/6/44
23. D
24. G
25. F
26. A
27. B
28. E
29. C

1/7/44 - 2/28/44
30. E
31. A
32. G
33. F
34. B
35. I
36. H
37. C
38. D

3/1/44 - 3/31/44
39. C
40. E
41. A
42. D
43. F
44. B

4/1/44 - 8/1/44
45. C
46. E
47. A
48. F
49. D
50. B

DAILY LESSONS

LESSON ONE

Objectives
1. To give students background information for *Anne Frank: Diary* . . .
2. To give students the opportunity to fulfill their nonfiction reading assignment that goes along with this unit
3. To give students practice using library resources
4. To prepare students for the introductory activity in Lesson Two

Activity
Assign one of each of the following topics to each of your students. Distribute Writing Assignment #1. Discuss the directions in detail. Take your students to the library so they may work on the assignment. Students should fill out a "Nonfiction Assignment Sheet" for at least one of the sources they used, and students should submit these sheets with their compositions.

Topics
1. Write a short biography of Adolf Hitler.
2. What was the significance of yellow stars, and why did Hitler make Jews wear them?
3. What was the SS/Gestapo?
4. What is Whitsun Day?
5. What's the Atlantic Wall?
6. What is Eldorado?
7. What is Zionism?
8. What is Fascism?
9. Who was Goebbels?
10. Who was Rauter?
11. What were concentration camps? What went on there?
12. Tell about three different Greek gods.
13. Tell about three different Roman gods.
14. What was the role of the Netherlands in World War II?
15. What was the role of Germany in World War II?
16. What was the role of the United States in World War II?
17. What were/are Nazis?
18. What are the main beliefs of the Jewish religion?
19. Who was Winston Churchill?
20. Give a biography of Dwight D. Eisenhower.
21. What is a diary?
22. Who were the Allies in World War II?
23. What was "D-Day"?
24. Why were Jewish people persecuted by Hitler's regime?
25. Who was DeGaulle of France?

WRITING ASSIGNMENT #1 - *Anne Frank: Diary*

PROMPT

You are going to read about Anne Frank, a 13 year-old Jewish girl who, with her family, went into hiding during World War II. It is a true story in Anne's own words; in fact, it is from her own personal diary. Before you read it, however, you should have some background information about some of the things Anne talks about in her diary.

You have been assigned one topic about which you must find information. You are to read as much as you can about that topic and write a composition in which you relate what you have learned from your reading. Note that this is a *composition*, not just a sentence or two.

PREWRITING

You will go to the library. When you get there, use the library's resources to find information about your topic. Look for books, encyclopedias, articles in magazines--anything that will give you the information you require. Take a few notes as you read to help you remember important dates, names, places, or other details that will be important in your composition.

After you have gathered information and become well-read on the subject of your report, make a little outline, putting your facts in order.

DRAFTING

You will need an introductory paragraph in which you introduce your topic.

In the body of your composition, put the "meat" of your research--the facts you found--in paragraph form. Each paragraph should have a topic sentence (a sentence letting the reader know what that paragraph will be about) followed by an explanation, examples or details.

Write a concluding paragraph in which you summarize the information you found and conclude your report.

PROMPT

When you finish the rough draft of your paper, ask a student who sits near you to read it. After reading your rough draft, he/she should tell you what he/she liked best about your work, which parts were difficult to understand, and ways in which your work could be improved. Reread your paper considering your critic's comments, and make the corrections you think are necessary.

PROOFREADING

Do a final proofreading of your paper double-checking your grammar, spelling, organization, and the clarity of your ideas.

NONFICTION ASSIGNMENT SHEET
(To be completed after reading the required nonfiction article)

Name _____ Date _____

Title of Nonfiction Read _____

Written By _____ Publication Date _____

I. Factual Summary: Write a short summary of the piece you read.

II. Vocabulary
    1. With which vocabulary words in the piece did you encounter some degree of difficulty?

    2. How did you resolve your lack of understanding with these words?

III. Interpretation: What was the main point the author wanted you to get from reading his work?

IV. Criticism
    1. With which points of the piece did you agree or find easy to accept? Why?

    2. With which points of the piece did you disagree or find difficult to believe? Why?

V. Personal Response: What do you think about this piece? OR How does this piece influence your ideas?

LESSON TWO

Objectives
1. To introduce the *Anne Frank: Diary of a Young Girl* unit
2. To distribute books and other related materials (study guides, reading assignments, etc)
3. To give students the opportunity to express their personal opinions
4. To show students what it was like for Anne to use her diary as a "patient listener" and "friend"

Note: Prior to this class period, you need to have put up a bulletin board titled: THE FACTS BEHIND *ANNE FRANK: DIARY OF A YOUNG GIRL* (or some other appropriate title). If you do not have a bulletin board to use, pass around a sheet of paper for students to write their facts on--and then make a copy of the page(s) for all your students to have for study purposes and reference.

Activity #1
Have each student go to the bulletin board and write one fact he/she learned from his/her research. Discuss each fact as it is presented so students will all be exposed to a wide variety of background information prior to reading *Anne Frank: Diary* . . . .

Activity #2
Distribute the materials students will use in this unit. Explain in detail how students are to use these materials.

Study Guides Students should read the study guide questions for each reading assignment prior to beginning the reading assignment to get a feeling for what events and ideas are important in the section they are about to read. After reading the section, students will (as a class or individually) answer the questions to review the important events and ideas from that section of the diary. Students should keep the study guides as study materials for the unit test.

Vocabulary Prior to reading a reading assignment, students will do vocabulary work related to the section of the diary they are about to read. Following the completion of the reading of the diary, there will be a vocabulary review of all the words used in the vocabulary assignments. Students should keep their vocabulary work as study materials for the unit test.

Reading Assignment Sheet You need to fill in the reading assignment sheet to let students know by when their reading has to be completed. You can either write the assignment sheet up on a side blackboard or bulletin board and leave it there for students to see each day, or you can "ditto" copies for each student to have. In either case, you should advise students to become very familiar with the reading assignments so they know what is expected of them.

<u>Extra Activities Center</u> The Extra Activities portion of this unit contains suggestions for an extra library of related books and articles in your classroom as well as crossword and word search puzzles. Make an extra activities center in your room where you will keep these materials for students to use. (Bring the books and articles in from the library and keep several copies of the puzzles on hand.) Explain to students that these materials are available for students to use when they finish reading assignments or other class work early.

<u>Books</u> Each school has its own rules and regulations regarding student use of school books. Advise students of the procedures that are normal for your school.

<u>Activity #3</u>
Distribute Writing Assignment #2. Discuss the directions in detail. Tell students that the diaries will be collected during Lesson Fifteen. (Give students the day/date.)

Note: The title of this book will hereafter occasionally be referred to as *Anne Frank: Diary*.

WRITING ASSIGNMENT #2 - *Anne Frank: Diary*

PROMPT
Anne was lonesome for a "special friend," someone with whom she could share her confidences, her secrets, her thoughts and personal feelings. The trouble was that she didn't think she had such a friend. So, when a diary (a blank book) appeared on her thirteenth birthday, she promptly named it "Kitty" and began to pour out her thoughts onto the pages.

Sometimes it's easier to put our feelings down on paper in a diary or in a letter to a friend than to actually *say* what's on our minds. Maybe it's a little less embarrassing; maybe it gives us a little extra time to think through our emotions or to find the right words--whatever the reasons, writing is often a good outlet when we're feeling lonely, confused, depressed, or even when we're really happy about something and there's no one around to tell!

Your assignment is to keep a diary for about three weeks. Each entry must be at least a good paragraph long (6-8 sentences). You may make your entries longer if you want. You must have an entry for at least five days out of each seven-day week. (A total of 15 entries is the minimum requirement.)

PREWRITING
What will you write about? Sit down somewhere quiet, someplace where you'll have some privacy. What's on your mind? What have you been thinking about lately? Your topics can be anything from simply telling what you did during the day, to discussing something that's bothering you, to writing about something you read or saw--really anything that comes to mind.

DRAFTING
What is important is that you sit down and write a little bit each day. Diaries are not formal, written papers; they are a form for personal expression. There is no right or wrong thing to include in your diary. There is no formal structure--no need for footnotes, quotations, or factual support for your statements. Just put pen to paper and write what you want to write. As you read Anne Frank's diary, you'll get the idea.

PROOFREADING
Anne often went back and reread her earlier entries--not so much for proofreading purposes since she never intended anyone else to read her diary, but just to see how her own thoughts and feelings had changed. Sometimes that rereading process can be as helpful as the writing process was. We may write something in haste or anger and go back a few days later, reread it, and think, "Gee! I can't believe I felt that way!" Proofreading in a diary should be more properly called "rereading," since there is no real need to correct your grammar.

LESSON THREE

Objectives
1. To read Reading Assignment #1
2. To give students practice reading orally
3. To evaluate students' oral reading
4. To preview the study questions for the first two reading assignments
5. To familiarize students with the vocabulary for Reading Assignment #1

Activity #1
Give students about fifteen minutes to preview the study questions for the first two reading assignments and to do the vocabulary worksheet for Reading Assignment #1.

Activity #2
Have students read Reading Assignment #1 of *Anne Frank: Diary of a Young Girl* out loud in class. You probably know the best way to get readers with your class; pick students at random, ask for volunteers, or use whatever method works best for your group. Have each student read one diary entry. If you have not yet completed an oral reading evaluation for your students this marking period, this would be a good opportunity to do so. A form is included with this unit for your convenience.

If students do not complete reading assignment 1 in class, they should do so prior to your next class meeting.

LESSON FOUR

Objectives
1. To read Reading Assignment #2
2. To give students practice reading orally
3. To evaluate students' oral reading
4. To familiarize students with the vocabulary in Reading Assignment #2

Activity #1
Give students about ten minutes to do the vocabulary worksheet for Reading Assignment #2.

Activity #2
Have students read Reading Assignment #2 of *Anne Frank: Diary of a Young Girl* out loud in class. Have each student read one diary entry. Continue the oral reading evaluations.

If students do not complete Reading Assignment 1 in class, they should do so prior to your next class meeting.

ORAL READING EVALUATION - *Anne Frank Diary of a Young Girl*

Name _____ Class____ Date _____

SKILL	EXCELLENT	GOOD	AVERAGE	FAIR	POOR
Fluency	5	4	3	2	1
Clarity	5	4	3	2	1
Audibility	5	4	3	2	1
Pronunciation	5	4	3	2	1
_____	5	4	3	2	1
_____	5	4	3	2	1

Total _____   Grade _____

Comments:

LESSON FIVE

Objectives
1. To review the main events and ideas from reading assignments 1 & 2
2. To preview the study questions for the remainder of the book
3. To familiarize students with the vocabulary in reading assignments 3 & 4
4. To read reading assignments 3 & 4

Activity #1

Give students a few minutes to formulate answers for the study guide questions for reading assignments 1 & 2, and then discuss the answers to the questions in detail. Write the answers on the board or overhead transparency so students can have the correct answers for study purposes. Note: It is a good practice in public speaking and leadership skills for individual students to take charge of leading the discussions of the study questions. Perhaps a different student could go to the front of the class and lead the discussion each day that the study questions are discussed during this unit. Of course, the teacher should guide the discussion when appropriate and be sure to fill in any gaps the students leave.

Activity #2

Give students about fifteen minutes to preview the study questions for the remainder of *Anne Frank: Diary of a Young Girl* and to do the related vocabulary work for Reading Assignment #3.

Activity #3

If you have given each student a grade for oral reading, have students read silently during this period. If students are reading silently, this would be a good time to have writing conferences with students about Writing Assignment #1. An evaluation form is provided in this unit to help you structure your writing conferences. If you have not completed the oral reading evaluations, do so during this class period.

Activity #4

Tell students that prior to Lesson Eight (give students a day/date), they should complete the reading and vocabulary work through Reading Assignment #4.

LESSON SIX

Objectives
    1. To tie Anne Frank's diary to something in students' real lives today
    2. To give students some practical, useful information they can use

Note: Prior to this class period, you need to find and schedule a guest speaker to come talk with your students.
    As you know, the Franks were totally dependent on a few close friends and associates for their daily necessities. There may be some students in your class who are in that situation, but most are not. There are, however, a growing number of people who are homeless or are just plain poor--don't have enough money to keep a lot of clothes in the closet or a lot of food on the table.
    This activity is intended to help students who are in that situation now--or students who may someday be in that situation. (We never know where life will take us!) Most teachers are on pretty tight budgets themselves!

Activity
    Have a guest speaker come talk with your students about how to make ends meet when there isn't enough money--ways to stretch the family budget. Your speaker could address many different areas of daily life from ways to save on transportation and clothing to ways to make your food budget stretch by shopping smarter and by using recipes that are delicious, nutritious and filling but relatively inexpensive.
    Check with social services or some other government or consumer agencies to see if they have a person trained in this area of expertise.

LESSON SEVEN

Objectives
1. To try out and put into practice some of the tips the guest speaker gave
2. To give students practical experience

Activity #1

Tell students that in Lesson Seven (give students a day/date), your class will have "Potato Day." What in the world is "Potato Day," they may ask. (And so might you at this point!) Well, potatoes and rice are staples that are almost always relatively inexpensive, are filling and nutritious. So, we're going to put our thinking caps on, drag out the dusty recipe box, and find creative ways to use these fantastic foods! There are two ways you could do this activity:

OPTION ONE: Have each student write down on a 3 X 5 card (or 1/2 sheet of paper) a recipe in which potatoes or rice are the main ingredients. On Potato Day, all students will bring in their recipes, and you'll spend some time discussing the wide variety of possibilities. Follow up by printing all the recipes in a little booklet and giving a booklet to each student.

OPTION TWO: Do Option One, but also have students make the dishes that they have the recipes for and bring them to class for everyone to taste. Follow up as in Option One.

Activity #2

Divide students into groups of four. (This activity could also be done individually.) Tell each group of four students that it has $100.00 with which to feed a family of four for one week. Tell the group to write out what the meals will be (breakfast, lunch and dinner) for seven days. (A chart will do.) Students must include a grocery list showing what they will need to buy to make these meals, and the approximate cost of each item. Students may assume the cupboard is already stocked with basics such as salt, pepper, condiments, and the usual spices. Everything else, including beverages and any dessert makings must be taken out of the $100.00. The four family members are a father, mother, teenager and eight year-old.

LESSON EIGHT

Objectives
    1. To familiarize students with the vocabulary in Reading Assignment #5
    2. To read Reading Assignment #5

Activity #1
    Give students about 10 minutes to do the prereading vocabulary work for Reading Assignment 5.

Activity #2
    Have students read Reading Assignment #5 silently for the remainder of the class period. If students do not complete reading these chapters during this class period, they should do so prior to your next class meeting.

LESSON NINE

Objectives
    1. To familiarize students with the vocabulary in Reading Assignment #6
    2. To read Reading Assignment #6

Activity #1
    Give students about 10 minutes to do the prereading vocabulary work for Reading Assignment 6.

Activity #2
    Have students read Reading Assignment #6 silently for the remainder of the class period. If students do not complete reading these chapters during this class period, they should do so prior to your next class meeting.

LESSON TEN

Objectives
1. To complete the recipe assignment made in Lesson Seven
2. To preview the vocabulary words in Reading Assignment 7
3. To read Reading Assignment 7

Activity #1
Have your "Potato Day" as discussed in Lesson Seven, either as Option One (having students share recipes) or Option Two (having students share recipes and bring in the prepared food to taste). In both circumstances, be sure to make a little recipe book for each student to have.

Activity #2
Tell students that prior to your next class meeting, they should have completed the vocabulary and reading work for Reading Assignment 7. If time remains in this period, students may begin working on this assignment.

LESSON ELEVEN

Objectives
1. To review the main ideas and events from Reading Assignments 3-7
2. To discuss *Anne Frank: Diary of a Young Girl* on interpretive and critical levels

Activity #1
Take a few minutes at the beginning of the period to review the study questions for Reading Assignments 3-7.

Activity #2
Choose the questions from the Extra Discussion Questions/Writing Assignments which seem most appropriate for your students. A class discussion of these questions is most effective if students have been given the opportunity to formulate answers to the questions prior to the discussion. To this end, you may either have all the students formulate answers to all the questions, divide your class into groups and assign one or more questions to each group, or you could assign one question to each student in your class. The option you choose will make a difference in the amount of class time needed for this activity.

Activity #3
After students have had ample time to formulate answers to the questions, begin your class discussion of the questions and the ideas presented by the questions. Be sure students take notes during the discussion so they have information to study for the unit test.

EXTRA WRITING ASSIGNMENTS/DISCUSSION QUESTIONS
Anne Frank: Diary of a Young Girl

Interpretation

1. What are the main conflicts in Anne Frank's diary? Are they resolved? How, or why not?

2. Does the fact that Anne Frank's diary is nonfiction change the way we are affected by the book? Why or why not?

3. Is there a climax in the diary? If so, where? If not, why not?

4. When and where do the events in the diary take place?

Critical

5. Explain how there are "Two Annes."

6. Discus the role of education in the life of Anne Frank.

7. Do any of the people mentioned in the diary change? If so, who and how?

8. Is the diary a tragedy in the literary sense of the word? Why or why not?

9. Characterize the relationship between Mr. and Mrs. Frank.

10. Characterize the relationship between Mr. and Mrs. Van Daan.

11. Characterize the relationship between Anne and Margot.

12. Characterize the relationship between Anne and Peter.

13. Characterize the relationship between Anne and Daddy.

14. Characterize the relationship between Anne and Mummy.

15. Is there any humor in Anne's diary? What effect does that have on our perception of Anne Frank and her situation?

16. What ideas in the diary are universal and ageless?

17. What is Anne's "war within"?

18. What were Anne's best qualities? Her worst?

19. Describe the role of religion in Anne Frank's life.

Anne Frank: Diary Extra Discussion Questions Page 2

20. Why did Anne Frank write a diary?

21. Lots of people keep diaries, and many other people did during the same period as Anne Frank. Why is Anne Frank's diary so widely read? What makes it so special?

22. Define "heroism" as it relates to Anne Frank's diary.

Personal Response

23. Could the same thing happen that happened to Anne's family happen in our world today? Explain why or why not.

24. How would the effect of Anne's diary have changed if she and her family had survived?

25. Did you enjoy reading *Anne Frank: Diary of a Young Girl*? Why or why not?

26. Why did Anne often mention that she was actually fortunate to be in hiding? What positive things came from being in hiding?

27. Suppose you and your family were thrust into the same situation as the Franks. Compare and contrast how you think your family would have reacted with the way the Franks did.

28. There were frightening things going on in Anne's world--the war and knowing that if she and her family were found, they would probably die. And yet, the Franks got up every morning and tried to make the best of their situation. There are frightening things going on in our world, in our cities, perhaps even in your own neighborhoods. And yet, we all get up each morning and make the best of our situations. Why?

29. Have you heard of or read any other stories of people who have been in hiding, persecuted, or surrounded by war? What were they?

30. Are there still places today where Jewish people are persecuted? If so, where and why?

31. In her diary Anne Frank mentions "The Art of Living." What does that mean?

LESSON TWELVE

Objective
> To review all of the vocabulary work done in this unit

Activity
> Choose one (or more) of the vocabulary review activities listed below and spend your class period as directed in the activity. Some of the materials for these review activities are located in the Extra Activities Packet in this unit.

VOCABULARY REVIEW ACTIVITIES

1. Divide your class into two teams and have an old-fashioned spelling or definition bee.

2. Give each of your students (or students in groups of two, three or four) a *Anne Frank: Diary of a Young Girl* Vocabulary Word Search Puzzle. The person (group) to find all of the vocabulary words in the puzzle first wins.

3. Give students a *Anne Frank: Diary of a Young Girl* Vocabulary Word Search Puzzle without the word list. The person or group to find the most vocabulary words in the puzzle wins.

4. Use a *Anne Frank: Diary of a Young Girl* Vocabulary Crossword Puzzle. Put the puzzle onto a transparency on the overhead projector (so everyone can see it), and do the puzzle together as a class.

5. Give students a *Anne Frank: Diary of a Young Girl* Vocabulary Matching Worksheet to do.

6. Divide your class into two teams. Use the *Anne Frank: Diary of a Young Girl* vocabulary words with their letters jumbled as a word list. Student 1 from Team A faces off against Student 1 from Team B. You write the first jumbled word on the board. The first student (1A or 1B) to unscramble the word wins the chance for his/her team to score points. If 1A wins the jumble, go to student 2A and give him/her a definition. He/she must give you the correct spelling of the vocabulary word which fits that definition. If he/she does, Team A scores a point, and you give student 3A a definition for which you expect a correctly spelled matching vocabulary word. Continue giving Team A definitions until some team member makes an incorrect response. An incorrect response sends the game back to the jumbled-word face off, this time with students 2A and 2B. Instead of repeating giving definitions to the first few students of each team, continue with the student after the one who gave the last incorrect response on the team. For example, if Team B wins the jumbled-word face-off, and student 5B gave the last incorrect answer for Team B, you would start this round of definition questions with student 6B, and so on. The team with the most points wins!

7. Have students write a story in which they correctly use as many vocabulary words as possible. Have students read their compositions orally! Post the most original compositions on your bulletin board.

LESSON THIRTEEN

Objective
	To study and discuss several quotations taken from Anne Frank's diary as a way of looking more closely at the ideas Anne presented in her diary

Activity
	Distribute the Quotations Worksheets. (It will help if you make a transparency for yourself of this, the study guide questions and the Extra Discussion Questions pages. If you use the overhead projector for these, you'll be able to face the class to lead the discussion and won't be covered from head to toe in chalk dust at the end of the class period.)
	Use the worksheets as a springboard for discussions about the ideas presented by the quotations.
	Student should write notes on their paper copies of the worksheets for study use later.

LESSONS FOURTEEN AND FIFTEEN

Objectives
	1. To further discuss the ideas presented in the diary
	2. To give students a chance to work together in small groups to exchange ideas and find information

Activity #1
	Divide your class into four groups--one group for each of the following topics:
	1. The diary as a portrait of war
	2. The diary as a philosophy of life
	3. The diary as a portrait of adolescence
	4. The diary as a study of the nature of people

	Students within the group should prepare to "teach" their topic as it relates to *Anne Frank: Diary*. They should find any relevant passages from the text and come to some reasonable conclusions about their topic as it relates to the book. One student in the group should be appointed secretary/spokesperson to write down and report the group's ideas. Give students ample time to gather information and think about their topics. Depending on the level of your class, allow at least 30 minutes for this part of the activity.

Activity #2
	Call on the groups to report the information they were able to compile. Jot the main points down briefly for students to copy into their notes. Use this as a springboard to discuss each of the topics above.

Activity #3
	In Lesson Fifteen, collect students' diaries (Writing Assignment 2).

QUOTATIONS WORKSHEET - *Anne Frank: The Diary of a Young Girl*

Explain the significance of the following quotations:

1. By tomorrow they would look just as filthy and ragged as before. (12/13/42)

2. This is exactly what the frightful puppet show on the radio was like. The wounded seemed to be proud of their wounds--the more the better. (3/19/43)

3. I can only feel sorry for Mummy, who has now had to discover that I have adopted her own attitude. (4/2/43)

4. A person of fifty-four who is still so pedantic and small-minded must be so by nature, and will never improve. (7/13/43)

5. When he reads, he has a deep wrinkle at the back of his head, but if he helps prepare potatoes, ... then it seems as if nothing else penetrates. Then he has on his "potato face," .... (8/18/43)

6. "Oh, if only the black circle could recede and open the way for us!" (11/8/43)

7. And I cannot help her, I can only look on, how others suffer and die, and can only pray to God to send her back to us. (11/27/43)

8. Now that is all very fine, but still, a friend can't take a mother's place. I need my mother as an example which I can follow, I want to be able to respect her. (1/5/44)

9. Then Granny appeared as a guardian angel; then followed Lies, who seems to be a symbol to me of the sufferings of all my girl friends and all Jews. (1/6/44)

Anne Frank: Diary Quotations Worksheet Page 2

10. I think it's all to the good to have learned a bit about human beings, but now I think I've learned enough. The war goes on just the same, whether or not we choose to quarrel, or long for freedom and fresh air, and so we should try to make the best of our stay here. (1/15/44)

11. I wonder whether you can tell me why it is that people always try so hard to hide their real feelings? How is it that I always behave quite differently from what I should in other people's company? Why do we trust one another so little? I know there must be a reason, but still I sometimes think it's horrible that you find you can never really confide in people, even in those who are nearest to you. (1/22/44)

12. I want to examine the whole matter carefully myself and find out what is true and what is exaggerated. (1/22/44)

13. ... it is impossible for anything in the conversation here to be fresh or new. (1/28/44)

14. Little children such as Anne must never, under any circumstances, know better than the grownups, however many blunders they make, and to whatever extent they allow their imaginations to run away with them. (1/28/44)

Anne Frank: Diary Quotations Worksheet Page 3

15. I have now reached the stage that I don't care much whether I live or die. The world will still keep on turning without me; what is going to happen, will happen, and anyway it's no good to resist. (2/3/44)

16. The best remedy for those who are afraid, lonely, or unhappy is to go outside , somewhere where they can be quite alone with the heavens, nature, and God. . . . I firmly believe that nature brings solace in all troubles. (2/23/44)

17. Riches can all be lost, but that happiness in your own heart can only be veiled, and it will still bring you happiness again, as long as you live. (2/23/44)

18. It was a good thing that in the midst of it, at the height of all this gaiety, I suddenly had to face reality, and it took me at least a year to get used to the fact that there was no more admiration forthcoming. (3/7/44)

19. I don't want followers, but friends, admirers who fall not for a flattering smile but for what one does and for one's character. (3/7/44)

20. I don't believe that the big men, the politicians and the capitalists alone, are guilty of the war. Oh, no, the little man is just as guilty, otherwise the peoples of the world would have risen in revolt long ago! There's in people simply an urge to destroy, an urge to kill, to murder and rage, and until all mankind, without exception, undergoes a great change, wars will be waged, everything that has been built up, cultivated, and grown will be destroyed and disfigured, after which mankind will have to begin all over again. (5/3/44)

Anne Frank: Diary Quotations Worksheet Page 4

21. We all live, but we don't know the why or the wherefore. We all live with the object of being happy; our lives are all different and yet the same. We three have been brought up in good circles, we have the chance to learn, the possibility of attaining something, we have all reason to hope for much happiness, but ... we must earn it for ourselves. And that is never easy. You must work and do good, not be lazy and gamble, if you wish to earn happiness. Laziness may appear attractive, but work gives satisfaction. (7/6/44)

22. How noble and good everyone could be if, every evening before falling asleep, they were to recall to their minds the events of the whole day and consider exactly what has been good and bad. Then, without realizing it, you try to improve yourself at the start of each new day; of course, you achieve quite a lot in the course of time. (7/6/44)

LESSON SIXTEEN

Objectives
1. To give students the opportunity to practice writing to persuade
2. To review character motivations
3. To give the teacher a chance to evaluate students' individual writing
4. To evaluate students' understanding of the characters in the diary

Activity #1
Distribute Writing Assignment #3. Discuss the directions orally in detail. Allow the remaining class time for students to complete the activity. If students do not have enough class time to finish, the papers may be collected at the beginning of the next class period.

Activity #2
While students are doing Writing Assignment #3, call individual students to your desk or some other private place, and discuss their earlier writing assignments. Give each students a little writing conference during which you point out the good things he/she does in his/her writing and make suggestions about how his/her writing could be improved. A writing evaluation form is included with this unit for your convenience, to help you structure your writing conferences.

After evaluating students' writing, suggest that students should rewrite at least one assignment (probably Writing Assignment #1 for this unit), taking into consideration your suggestions for improvement. Tell students when these revisions will be due. When you grade the revisions, use an A-C-E kind of a scale. (A for all revisions made and a job well done, C for some revisions made, or E for no attempt made at the revisions.) This will greatly speed up grading time and still give students credit for their efforts.

LESSON SEVENTEEN

Objective
To review the main ideas presented in *Anne Frank: Diary of a Young Girl*

Activity #1
Choose one of the review games/activities included in Extra Activities section and spend your class period as outlined there. Some materials for these activities are located in the Extra Activities section of this unit.

Activity #2
Remind students that the Unit Test will be in the next class meeting. Stress the review of the Study Guides and their class notes as a last minute, brush-up review for homework.

WRITING ASSIGNMENT #3 - *Anne Frank: Diary*

PROMPT
You are Anne Frank. Your assignment is to persuade your mother to change her attitude towards you and to treat you as you would like to be treated.

PREWRITING
In order to do this assignment, you must understand Anne, Anne's perception of her mother, Anne's mother, and her perception of Anne. Make four columns on a blank sheet of paper, and label each of the columns with one of the things you must understand, just stated in the previous sentence. Under each heading, write down all the things you can think of that relate to it.

Now you need to write down how Anne's mother treats her. After that make notes about how Anne would like to be treated. You should find that these two groups of information contain pairs of opposites. For example, Anne's mother treats her like a child, and Anne would like her mother to treat her in a more adult fashion, etc. Find the pairs of opposites.

For each pair of opposites, write down reasons why Anne's mother should do what Anne would want her to do. For example, write down reasons why Anne's mother should treat Anne more like an adult.

DRAFTING
Write an introductory paragraph in which you (Anne) explain to your mother (Mrs. Frank) that you would like to be treated differently.

In the body of your composition, write one paragraph for each of the "pairs of opposites" you found in your prewriting exercise. In each paragraph, write a topic sentence in which you state to your mother one way she treats you and how you would like her to treat you differently. For example, let her know that you feel she treats you like a child and that you would like to be treated more like an adult. After your topic sentence, fill out your paragraph with examples and reasons why your mother should change her behavior towards you on this point.

After you have written one paragraph for each of the pairs of opposites, write a concluding paragraph in which you summarize your points and make your concluding remarks.

PROMPT
When you finish the rough draft of your paper, ask a student who sits near you to read it. After reading your rough draft, he/she should tell you what he/she liked best about your work, which parts were difficult to understand, and ways in which your work could be improved. Reread your paper considering your critic's comments and make the corrections you think are necessary.

PROOFREADING
Do a final proofreading of your paper double-checking your grammar, spelling, organization, and the clarity of your ideas.

WRITING EVALUATION FORM - *Anne Frank: Diary of a Young Girl*

Name _____ Date _____

Grade _____

Circle One For Each Item:

Grammar: corrections noted on paper

Spelling: corrections noted on paper

Punctuation: corrections noted on paper

Legibility: excellent   good   fair   poor

Strengths:

Weaknesses:

Comments/Suggestions:

REVIEW GAMES/ACTIVITIES - *Anne Frank: Diary of a Young Girl*

1. Ask the class to make up a unit test for *Anne Frank: Diary of a Young Girl*. The test should have 4 sections: matching, true/false, short answer, and essay. Students may use 1/2 period to make the test and then swap papers and use the other 1/2 class period to take a test a classmate has devised (open book). You may want to use the unit test included in this section or take questions from the students' unit tests to formulate your own test.

2. Take 1/2 period for students to make up true and false questions (including the answers). Collect the papers and divide the class into two teams. Draw a big tic-tac-toe board on the chalk board. Make one team X and one team O. Ask questions to each side, giving each student one turn. If the question is answered correctly, that students' team's letter (X or O) is placed in the box. If the answer is incorrect, no mark is placed in the box. The object is to get three marks in a row like tic-tac-toe. You may want to keep track of the number of games won for each team.

3. Take 1/2 period for students to make up questions (true/false and short answer). Collect the questions. Divide the class into two teams. You'll alternate asking questions to individual members of teams A & B (like in a spelling bee). The question keeps going from A to B until it is correctly answered, then a new question is asked. A correct answer does not allow the team to get another question. Correct answers are +2 points; incorrect answers are -1 point.

4. Have students pair up and quiz each other from their study guides and class notes.

5. Give students a *Anne Frank: Diary of a Young Girl* crossword puzzle to complete.

6. Divide your class into two teams. Use the *Anne Frank: Diary of a Young Girl* crossword words with their letters jumbled as a word list. Student 1 from Team A faces off against Student 1 from Team B. You write the first jumbled word on the board. The first student (1A or 1B) to unscramble the word wins the chance for his/her team to score points. If 1A wins the jumble, go to student 2A and give him/her a clue. He/she must give you the correct word which matches that clue. If he/she does, Team A scores a point, and you give student 3A a clue for which you expect another correct response. Continue giving Team A clues until some team member makes an incorrect response. An incorrect response sends the game back to the jumbled-word face off, this time with students 2A and 2B. Instead of repeating giving clues to the first few students of each team, continue with the student after the one who gave the last incorrect response on the team. For example, if Team B wins the jumbled-word face-off, and student 5B gave the last incorrect answer for Team B, you would start this round of clue questions with student 6B, and so on. The team with the most points wins!

LESSON EIGHTEEN

Objective
To test the students' understanding of the main ideas and themes in *Anne Frank: Diary of a Young Girl*

Activity #1
Distribute the unit tests. Go over the instructions in detail and allow the students the entire class period to complete the exam.

NOTES ABOUT THE UNIT TESTS IN THIS UNIT:

There are 5 different unit tests which follow.

There are two short answer tests which are based primarily on facts from the diary.

There is one advanced short answer unit test. It is based on the extra discussion questions and quotations. Use the matching key for short answer unit test 2 to check the matching section of the advanced short answer unit test. There is no key for the short answer questions and quotations. The answers will be based on the discussions you have had during class.

There are two multiple choice unit tests. Following the two unit tests, you will find an answer sheet on which students should mark their answers. Following the students' answer sheet for the multiple choice tests you will find your answer keys.

The short answer tests have a vocabulary section. You should choose 10 of the vocabulary words from this unit, read them orally and have the students write them down. Then, either have students write a definition or use the words in sentences.

Use these words for the vocabulary section of the advanced short answer unit test:

ardent	boisterous	clandestine	congenial
impertinent	inevitably	loathe	procured
rebuke	superfluous	tact	vague

Activity #2
Collect all test papers and assigned books prior to the end of the class period.

UNIT TESTS

SHORT ANSWER UNIT TEST 1 - *Anne Frank: Diary of a Young Girl*

I. Matching/Identify

____ 1. Dussel   A. She and Meip help keep spirits up

____ 2. Elli   B. Peter's cat

____ 3. Henk   C. Assumed Mr. Frank's business responsibilities

____ 4. Hitler   D. Elderly dentist who shares Anne's room

____ 5. Kitty   E. He was esp. helpful in getting food and arranging logistics

____ 6. Kolen   F. Office worker; she brought news and presents

____ 7. Koophuis   G. Anne's sister

____ 8. Kraler   H. Anne and Margot exchanged letters about him

____ 9. Lies   I. Leader of Nazi Germany

____ 10. Margot   J. Family living with the Franks

____ 11. Meip   K. __ & Co.; firm in which Mr. Frank was a partner

____ 12. Mouschi   L. Anne saw her pleading, "Help, oh, help me . . ."

____ 13. Otto   M. Meip's husband

____ 14. Peter   N. Mr. Frank

____ 15. Van Daan   O. Anne's fictitious diary friend

Anne Frank: Diary of a Young Girl Short Answer Unit Test 1 Page 2

II. Short Answer

1. Who was Anne Frank?

2. What were some of the restrictions placed on the Dutch Jews by the Germans?

3. What forces the Franks into hiding?

4. What contact do the Franks and Van Daans have with the outside world?

5. As their first year in hiding draws to a close, two more disasters strike. Describe them. (June 15 entry)

6. Anne ends her third six months in hiding with an awakening maturity. What evidence of this growth is reported in her diary?

7. Although Anne is not much interested in politics, one entry in March of 1944 tells about the various opinions of the group. what are the prevailing viewpoints?

8. What momentous event occurred in June of 1944?

9. The diary ends on August 1, 1944. What happens to Anne and her "family"?

10. Who are the "protectors" of the Franks and Van Daans? What are their names and what do they do?

Anne Frank: Diary of a Young Girl Short Answer Unit Test 1 Page 3

III. Composition

    Anne Frank mentioned "The Art of Living." What is that, and how did her life exemplify it?

Anne Frank: Diary of a Young Girl Short Answer Unit Test 1 Page 4

IV. Vocabulary: Write the words which are given orally and then go back and write definitions for those words.

1.

2.

3.

4.

5.

6.

7.

8.

9.

10.

SHORT ANSWER UNIT TEST 2 - *Anne Frank: Diary of a Young Girl*

I. Matching

____ 1. Dussel   A. Leader of Nazi Germany

____ 2. Elli   B. Family living with the Franks

____ 3. Henk   C. __ & Co.; firm in which Mr. Frank was a partner

____ 4. Hitler   D. Anne saw her pleading, "Help, oh, help me . . ."

____ 5. Kitty   E. Meip's husband

____ 6. Kolen   F. Mr. Frank

____ 7. Koophuis   G. Office worker; she brought news and presents

____ 8. Kraler   H. Anne's fictitious diary friend

____ 9. Lies   I. She and Meip help keep spirits up

____ 10. Margot   J. Peter's cat

____ 11. Meip   K. Assumed Mr. Frank's business responsibilities

____ 12. Mouschi   L. Elderly dentist who shares Anne's room

____ 13. Otto   M. He was esp. helpful in getting food and arranging logistics

____ 14. Peter   N. Anne's sister

____ 15. Van Daan   O. Anne and Margot exchanged letters about him

Anne Frank: Diary of a Young Girl Short Answer Unit Test 2 Page 2

II. Short Answer: Explain the significance of the following quotations:

1. By tomorrow they would look just as filthy and ragged as before.

2. I can only feel sorry for Mummy, who has now had to discover that I have adopted her own attitude.

3. And I cannot help her, I can only look on, how others suffer and die, and can only pray to God to send her back to us.

4. Now that is all very fine, but still, a friend can't take a mother's place. I need my mother as an example which I can follow, I want to be able to respect her.

5. I think it's all to the good to have learned a bit about human beings, but now I think I've learned enough. The war goes on just the same, whether or not we choose to quarrel, or long for freedom and fresh air, and so we should try to make the best of our stay here.

6. I want to examine the whole matter carefully myself and find out what is true and what is exaggerated.

7. I have now reached the stage that I don't care much whether I live or die. The world will still keep on turning without me; what is going to happen, will happen, and anyway it's no good to resist.

Anne Frank: Diary of a Young Girl Short Answer Unit Test 2 Page 3

III. Composition

Anne Frank's diary ends with the words, ". . .[I] keep on trying to find a way of becoming what I would so like to be, and what I could be, if . . . there weren't any other people living in the world." Explain what Anne Frank meant by this statement in relation to the events she had narrated in her diary, and explain the irony of her statement knowing that soon after she wrote it she was taken to a concentration camp where she died.

Anne Frank: Diary of a Young Girl Short Answer Unit Test 2 Page 4

IV. Vocabulary
    Listen to the vocabulary words and write them down.
    Go back later and write down the definitions for the words.

1.

2.

3.

4.

5.

6.

7.

8.

9.

10.

KEY: SHORT ANSWER UNIT TESTS - *Anne Frank: Diary of a Young Girl*

The short answer questions are taken directly from the study guides. If you need to look up the answers, you will find them in the study guide section.

Answers to the composition questions will vary depending on your class discussions and the level of your students.

For the vocabulary section of the test, choose ten of the words from the vocabulary lists to read orally for your students.

The answers to the matching section of the test are below.

Answers to the matching section of the Advanced Short Answer Unit Test are the same as for Short Answer Unit Test #2.

Test #1	Test #2
1. D	1. L
2. A	2. I
3. M	3. E
4. I	4. A
5. O	5. H
6. K	6. C
7. E	7. M
8. C	8. K
9. L	9. D
10. G	10. N
11. F	11. G
12. B	12. J
13. N	13. F
14. H	14. O
15. J	15. B

ADVANCED SHORT ANSWER UNIT TEST - *Anne Frank: Diary of a Young Girl*

I. Matching

____ 1. Dussel	A. Leader of Nazi Germany

____ 2. Elli	B. Family living with the Franks

____ 3. Henk	C. __ & Co.; firm in which Mr. Frank was a partner

____ 4. Hitler	D. Anne saw her pleading, "Help, oh, help me . . ."

____ 5. Kitty	E. Meip's husband

____ 6. Kolen	F. Mr. Frank

____ 7. Koophuis	G. Office worker; she brought news and presents

____ 8. Kraler	H. Anne's fictitious diary friend

____ 9. Lies	I. She and Meip help keep spirits up

____ 10. Margot	J. Peter's cat

____ 11. Meip	K. Assumed Mr. Frank's business responsibilities

____ 12. Mouschi	L. Elderly dentist who shares Anne's room

____ 13. Otto	M. He was esp. helpful in getting food and arranging logistics

____ 14. Peter	N. Anne's sister

____ 15. Van Daan	O. Anne and Margot exchanged letters about him

Anne Frank: Diary of a Young Girl Advanced Short Answer Unit Test Page 2

II. Short Answer

1. Explain how there are "Two Annes."

2. Discuss Anne's development from the beginning to the end of her diary. How does she grow and change?

3. Describe Anne's relationship with her mother.

4. What was Anne's "war within"?

Anne Frank: Diary of a Young Girl Advanced Short Answer Unit Test Page 3

5. How did the Van Daans influence life in the annexe?

6. Give examples of three ideas in the diary that are universal and ageless.

7. Explain the significance of the following quotations:
    a. When he reads, he has a deep wrinkle at the back of his head, but if he helps prepare potatoes, . . . then it seems as if nothing else penetrates. Then he has on his "potato face . . . ."

    b. Little children such as Anne must never, under any circumstances, know better than the grownups, however many blunders they make, and to whatever extent they allow their imaginations to run away with them.

    c. The best remedy for those who are afraid, lonely, or unhappy is to go outside, somewhere where they can be quite alone with the heavens, nature, and God . . . . I firmly believe that nature brings solace in all troubles.

    d. Oh, no, the little man is just as guilty, otherwise the peoples of the world would have risen in revolt long ago!

Anne Frank: Diary of a Young Girl Advanced Short Answer Unit Test Page 4

III. Composition

"We all live, but we don't know the why or the wherefore. We all live with the object of being happy; our lives are all different and yet the same. We three have been brought up in good circles, we have the chance to learn, the possibility of attaining something, we have all reason to hope for much happiness, but . . . we must earn it for ourselves. And that is never easy. You must work and do good, not be lazy and gamble, if you wish to earn happiness. Laziness may appear attractive, but work gives satisfaction."

Explain all the ways this quote applies to Anne and her situation.

Anne Frank: Diary of a Young Girl Advanced Short Answer Unit Test Page 5

IV. Vocabulary

Listen to the vocabulary words and write them down. Go back later and write a composition using all of the words. The composition must relate to Anne Frank.

MULTIPLE CHOICE UNIT TEST 1 - *Anne Frank: Diary of a Young Girl*

I. Matching

____ 1. Dussel   A. She and Meip help keep spirits up

____ 2. Elli   B. Peter's cat

____ 3. Henk   C. Assumed Mr. Frank's business responsibilities

____ 4. Hitler   D. Elderly dentist who shares Anne's room

____ 5. Kitty   E. He was esp. helpful in getting food and arranging logistics

____ 6. Kolen   F. Office worker; she brought news and presents

____ 7. Koophuis   G. Anne's sister

____ 8. Kraler   H. Anne and Margot exchanged letters about him

____ 9. Lies   I. Leader of Nazi Germany

____ 10. Margot   J. Family living with the Franks

____ 11. Meip   K. __ & Co.; firm in which Mr. Frank was a partner

____ 12. Mouschi   L. Anne saw her pleading, "Help, oh, help me . . ."

____ 13. Otto   M. Meip's husband

____ 14. Peter   N. Mr. Frank

____ 15. Van Daan   O. Anne's fictitious diary friend

II. Multiple Choice
1. When does Anne's diary begin? Why is this day special?
    A. It begins on June 14, 1942, Anne's birthday.
    B. It begins on September 8, 1941, Anne's first day of high school.
    C. It begins on December 19, 1942, the first day of Hanukkah.
    D. It begins on February 21, 1941, the day of Anne's first date.

Anne Frank: Diary Multiple Choice Unit Test 1 Page 2

2. Which describes Anne's life prior to the beginning of the diary?
    A. She was born in London and moved to New Delhi when she was three. Her father was a colonel in the British Army.
    B. She was born in Frankfort, Germany. She moved to Holland when her father went into business there.
    C. She was born in New York. Her father wanted to become a landowner, and moved the family to Oregon on a wagon train.
    D. She was born in Paris. Her father was a political activist, and moved the family to South Africa so he could work for civil rights for the Blacks.

3. Which was not a restriction placed on the Dutch Jews by the Germans?
    A. Wearing a yellow star on all clothes
    B. Not riding their bicycles or driving
    C. Only speaking Hebrew
    D. Shopping between three and five o'clock in the afternoon

4. What forces the Franks into hiding?
    A. Margot receives a notice that she is to be deported to a concentration camp.
    B. The family does not have enough money to flee to America.
    C. Mr. Frank is suspected of visiting Christians.
    D. A neighbor is making up stories about them disobeying the restrictions.

5. Where is the secret annexe located?
    A. It is in the country, in a barn on Meip's father's farm.
    B. It is in downtown Amsterdam, in the building where Mr. Frank's office and warehouse were located.
    C. It is just outside the city, in an orphanage.
    D. It is in the city, in the church Mr. Kraler attends.

6. Which is not one of the clashes they have because of their confinement?
    A. Mr. and Mrs. Van Daan yell at each other.
    B. Anne and Margot vie for Peter's attention.
    C. Mrs. Van Daan shirks her dishwashing duties.
    D. Anne's chatter annoys the others.

7. Anne ends her third six months in hiding with an awakening maturity. Which is not a sign of her growth?
    A. She has started to write a novel.
    B. She realizes she has been cruel to her mother.
    C. She is becoming interested in the opposite sex.
    D. She shows a new appreciation for their protectors.

Anne Frank: Diary Multiple Choice Unit Test 1 Page 3

8. The diary ends on August 1, 1944. What happens to Anne and the others?
    A. They are rounded up by the Gestapo. All die except Mr. Frank.
    B. They leave the secret annexe. The Franks and Peter escape, but the others are caught.
    C. The protectors smuggle them all to safety in the country.
    D. They all commit suicide rather than surrender to the Germans.

9. What was the role of education in Anne Frank's life?
    a. She was uneducated; the war closed down all the schools.
    b. She hated school and wished she would never have to go back.
    c. She was well-read and well educated and continued her education in the annexe.
    d. She was well educated at school before going to the annexe, but she continued her education at the annexe only because her father demanded it.

10. What was the relationship between Anne and Margot?
    a. They were not friends and not enemies; they were just sisters.
    b. They were friends until they had a huge argument over which one would get Peter as a boyfriend.
    c. They were not only sisters; they were best friends.
    d. Each was so jealous of the other that they never had a chance to become close.

11. What ideas in the diary were universal and ageless?
    1. Young love
    2. The tragedy of war
    3. The nature of people
    4. The corrupting influences of money
    a. 1 & 4
    b. 2, 3, &4
    c. 1, 2, &3
    d. All

12. "By tomorrow they would look just as filthy and ragged as before."
    a. Anne was disgusted with the lower-class street children; actually, she was jealous of their freedom.
    b. Anne was depressed because the whole world seemed filthy and ragged; the children were just another reminder.
    c. Anne was commenting on the sameness, helplessness and the monotony of her situation. The children would be filthy and raggy tomorrow, the war would still be going on, and there would still be no end in sight to her situation.
    d. Anne was commenting on the relationships between the Jews and Christians. It wouldn't matter what one group would do for the other; they would always be at odds because of the nature of their differences.

Anne Frank: Diary Multiple Choice Unit Test 1 Page 4

13. "Little children such as Anne must never, under any circumstances, know better than the grownups, however many blunders they make, and to whatever extent they allow their imaginations to run away with them."
    a. Anne is talking to herself, tongue-in-cheek, mimicking what the grownups would say if she would speak her mind.
    b. Anne overheard a conversation between Mrs. Van Daan and Mummy, in which Mummy was expressing how exasperated she has become at Anne's behavior.
    c. Anne was crushed when she overheard Peter telling this to Margot.
    d. Ann totally lost her self-control in an argument with Mummy and said this. Mummy was at first mortified that little Anne would say such a thing to her, but she later decided that Anne, like the rest of the family had been under a lot of stress, and thought it best to forget it.

Anne Frank: Diary Multiple Choice Unit Test 1 Page 5

IV. Vocabulary - Match the correct definitions to the words

___ 1. PROCURED   A. Reserved; remote

___ 2. TACT   B. Troubled with uncertainty

___ 3. PERPLEXED   C. Only

___ 4. OBSTINATE   D. Ability to act or speak without offending

___ 5. ALOOF   E. Jumble of loud noises

___ 6. CONDOLE   F. Despicable; contemptible

___ 7. SOLE   G. To express sympathy

___ 8. FATALIST   H. Never to be forgotten

___ 9. SARCASM   I. To become dull or boring

___ 10. PALL   J. Unavoidably

___ 11. ADO   K. Fervent; passionate

___ 12. TOLERANT   L. Got by special effort; obtained

___ 13. CONCEITED   M. Characterized by holding an unusually high opinion of oneself

___ 14. COMPENSATION   N. Cutting remarks

___ 15. ARDENT   O. One who believes all events are predetermined and inevitable

___ 16. IMMORTAL   P. Provoked; full of resentment

___ 17. DISDAINFUL   Q. Stubborn

___ 18. INEVITABLY   R. Bustle; fuss; bother

___ 19. DIN   S. Offset; counterbalance; repayment

___ 20. PIQUED   T. Inclined to put up with beliefs, practices or traits of others

MULTIPLE CHOICE UNIT TEST 2 - *Anne Frank: Diary of a Young Girl*

I. Matching

____ 1. Dussel	A. Leader of Nazi Germany

____ 2. Elli	B. Family living with the Franks

____ 3. Henk	C. __ & Co.; firm in which Mr. Frank was a partner

____ 4. Hitler	D. Anne saw her pleading, "Help, oh, help me . . . "

____ 5. Kitty	E. Meip's husband

____ 6. Kolen	F. Mr. Frank

____ 7. Koophuis	G. Office worker; she brought news and presents

____ 8. Kraler	H. Anne's fictitious diary friend

____ 9. Lies	I. She and Meip help keep spirits up

____ 10. Margot	J. Peter's cat

____ 11. Meip	K. Assumed Mr. Frank's business responsibilities

____ 12. Mouschi	L. Elderly dentist who shares Anne's room

____ 13. Otto	M. He was esp. helpful in getting food and arranging logistics

____ 14. Peter	N. Anne's sister

____ 15. Van Daan	O. Anne and Margot exchanged letters about him

II. Multiple Choice
1. When does Anne's diary begin? Why is this day special?
    A. It begins on December 19, 1942, the first day of Hanukkah.
    B. It begins on September 8, 1941, Anne's first day of high school.
    C. It begins on June 14, 1942, Anne's birthday.
    D. It begins on February 21, 1941, the day of Anne's first date.

Anne Frank: Diary Multiple Choice Unit Test 2 Page 2

2. Which describes Anne's life prior to the beginning of the diary?
    A. She was born in Frankfort, Germany. She moved to Holland when her father went into business there.
    B. She was born in London and moved to New Delhi when she was three. Her father was a colonel in the British Army.
    C. She was born in New York. Her father wanted to become a landowner, and moved the family to Oregon on a wagon train.
    D. She was born in Paris. Her father was a political activist, and moved the family to South Africa so he could work for civil rights for the Blacks.

3. Which was not a restriction placed on the Dutch Jews by the Germans?
    A. Wearing a yellow star on all clothes
    B. Not riding their bicycles or driving
    C. Shopping between three and five o'clock in the afternoon
    D. Only speaking Hebrew

4. What forces the Franks into hiding?
    A. The family does not have enough money to flee to America.
    B. Margot receives a notice that she is to be deported to a concentration camp.
    C. Mr. Frank is suspected of visiting Christians.
    D. A neighbor is making up stories about them disobeying the restrictions.

5. Where is the secret annexe located?
    A. It is in the country, in a barn on Meip's father's farm.
    B. It is just outside the city, in an orphanage.
    C. It is in downtown Amsterdam, in the building where Mr. Frank's office and warehouse were located.
    D. It is in the city, in the church Mr. Kraler attends.

6. Which is not one of the clashes they have because of their confinement?
    A. Mr. and Mrs. Van Daan yell at each other.
    B. Mrs. Van Daan shirks her dishwashing duties.
    C. Anne and Margot vie for Peter's attention.
    D. Anne's chatter annoys the others.

7. Anne ends her third six months in hiding with an awakening maturity. Which is not a sign of her growth?
    A. She shows a new appreciation for their protectors.
    B. She realizes she has been cruel to her mother.
    C. She is becoming interested in the opposite sex.
    D. She has started to write a novel.

Anne Frank: Diary Multiple Choice Unit Test 2 Page 3

8. The diary ends on August 1, 1944. What happens to Anne and the others?
    A. They leave the secret annexe. The Franks and Peter escape, but the others are caught.
    B. They are rounded up by the Gestapo. All die except Mr. Frank.
    C. The protectors smuggle them all to safety in the country.
    D. They all commit suicide rather than surrender to the Germans.

9. What was the role of education in Anne Frank's life?
    a. She was well-read and well educated and continued her education in the annexe.
    b. She hated school and wished she would never have to go back.
    c. She was uneducated; the war closed down all the schools.
    d. She was well educated at school before going to the annexe, but she continued her education at the annexe only because her father demanded it.

10. What was the relationship between Anne and Margot?
    a. They were friends until they had a huge argument over which one would get Peter as a boyfriend.
    b. They were not friends and not enemies; they were just sisters.
    c. They were not only sisters; they were best friends.
    d. Each was so jealous of the other that they never had a chance to become close.

11. What ideas in the diary were universal and ageless?
    1. Young love
    2. The tragedy of war
    3. The nature of people
    4. The corrupting influences of money
    a. 1, 2, &3
    b. 2, 3, &4
    c. 1 & 4
    d. All

12. "By tomorrow they would look just as filthy and ragged as before."
    a. Anne was disgusted with the lower-class street children; actually, she was jealous of their freedom.
    b. Anne was depressed because the whole world seemed filthy and ragged; the children were just another reminder.
    c. Anne was commenting on the relationships between the Jews and Christians. It wouldn't matter what one group would do for the other; they would always be at odds because of the nature of their differences.
    d. Anne was commenting on the sameness, helplessness and the monotony of her situation. The children would be filthy and raggy tomorrow, the war would still be going on, and there would still be no end in sight to her situation.

Anne Frank: Diary Multiple Choice Unit Test 2 Page 4

13. "Little children such as Anne must never, under any circumstances, know better than the grownups, however many blunders they make, and to whatever extent they allow their imaginations to run away with them."
    a. Anne overheard a conversation between Mrs. Van Daan and Mummy, in which Mummy was expressing how exasperated she has become at Anne's behavior.
    b. Anne is talking to herself, tongue-in-cheek, mimicking what the grownups would say if she would speak her mind.
    c. Anne was crushed when she overheard Peter telling this to Margot.
    d. Anne totally lost her self-control in an argument with Mummy and said this. Mummy was at first mortified that little Anne would say such a thing to her, but she later decided that Anne, like the rest of the family had been under a lot of stress, and thought it best to forget it.

Anne Frank: Diary Multiple Choice Unit Test 2 Page 5

IV. Vocabulary - Match the correct definitions to the words.

___ 1. TINGE   A. A fictitious name used by an author

___ 2. BLISS   B. Friendly

___ 3. CONCEITED   C. Surrender under specified conditions

___ 4. LOATHE   D. Cutting remarks

___ 5. FATUOUS   E. Ability to act or speak without offending

___ 6. NUISANCE   F. To express sympathy

___ 7. SARCASM   G. Improperly forward or bold

___ 8. CONGENIAL   H. Foolish

___ 9. QUEERLY   I. Extreme happiness

___ 10. OPPRESSIVE   J. Not needed

___ 11. CONDOLE   K. Slight addition

___ 12. INEVITABLY   L. Unavoidably

___ 13. TACT   M. Characterized by holding an unusually high opinion of oneself

___ 14. CAPITULATION   N. Difficult to bear; weighing heavily on the spirit

___ 15. SUPERFLUOUS   O. Continually, without interruption

___ 16. PSEUDONYM   P. Reserved; remote

___ 17. IMPERTINENT   Q. Lack of basic necessities of life

___ 18. PRIVATIONS   R. Hate; extreme dislike

___ 19. INCESSANTLY   S. Bother

___ 20. ALOOF   T. Oddly

ANSWER SHEET - *Anne Frank: Diary of a Young Girl*
Multiple Choice Unit Test

I. Matching
1. ___
2. ___
3. ___
4. ___
5. ___
6. ___
7. ___
8. ___
9. ___
10. ___
11. ___
12. ___
13. ___
14. ___
15. ___

II. Multiple Choice
1. ___
2. ___
3. ___
4. ___
5. ___
6. ___
7. ___
8. ___
9. ___
10. ___
11. ___
12. ___
13. ___

III. Vocabulary
1. ___
2. ___
3. ___
4. ___
5. ___
6. ___
7. ___
8. ___
9. ___
10. ___
11. ___
12. ___
13. ___
14. ___
15. ___
16. ___
17. ___
18. ___
19. ___
20. ___

ANSWER SHEET KEY - *Anne Frank: Diary of a Young Girl*
Multiple Choice Unit Test 1

Unit Test 1 answers are in the left column. Unit Test 2 answers are in the right column.

I. Matching	II. Multiple Choice	III. Vocabulary
1. D L	1. A C	1. L B
2. A I	2. B A	2. D A
3. M E	3. C D	3. B C
4. I A	4. A B	4. Q A
5. O H	5. B C	5. A C
6. K C	6. B C	6. G B
7. E M	7. A D	7. C B
8. C K	8. A B	8. O C
9. L D	9. C A	9. N C
10. G N	10. A B	10. I D
11. F G	11. C A	11. R A
12. B J	12. C D	12. T B
13. N F	13. A A	13. M C
14. H O		14. S A
15. J B		15. K B
		16. H C
		17. F A
		18. J C
		19. E D
		20. P B

UNIT RESOURCE MATERIALS

BULLETIN BOARD IDEAS - *Anne Frank: Diary of a Young Girl*

1. Save one corner of the board for the best of students' *Anne Frank: Diary of a Young Girl* writing assignments.

2. Take one of the word search puzzles from the extra activities packet and with a marker copy it over in a large size on the bulletin board. Write the clue words to find to one side. Invite students prior to and after class to find the words and circle them on the bulletin board.

3. Make a bulletin board about famous young people; young people who have enriched our lives either by their writing, like Anne, acting, or in any other way they may have contributed to our society.

4. Make a bulletin board listing the vocabulary words for this unit. As you complete sections of the diary and discuss the vocabulary for each section, write the definitions on the bulletin board. (If your board is one students face frequently, it will help them learn the words.)

5. Post a map of Europe (as it was in WWII) and place cut-out stars on the places mentioned in the diary.

6. Make a bulletin board about things one can do when one is stuck inside in a confined area. Either write up your own ideas or get students to write up theirs.

7. Title the board: ANNE FRANK:DIARY OF A YOUNG GIRL. Take a marker and write up several of the most interesting of Anne's diary entries.

8. Make a bulletin board about hotlines people can call when they don't have friends to talk to or when they are having trouble at home.

9. Have students make lists or bring pictures of three things they would most want to take with them if they had to leave their homes and go into hiding. Have each student tell why he/she chose the items he/she did, and have students post their lists on the bulletin board. Title the board: YOU CAN'T TAKE IT ALL WITH YOU or some other appropriate title.

10. Do a bulletin board about budgeting and making a little money or a little food stretch to be enough to provide the basics.

11. Make a bulletin board explaining the basic principles of Judaism.

12. Make a bulletin board advertising reading as a form of education.

13. Make a bulletin board about professional writers, careers in writing or how to become a successful author.

EXTRA ACTIVITIES

One of the difficulties in teaching a novel is that all students don't read at the same speed. One student who likes to read may take the book home and finish it in a day or two. Sometimes a few students finish the in-class assignments early. The problem, then, is finding suitable extra activities for students.

The best thing I've found is to keep a little library in the classroom. For this unit on *Anne Frank: Diary of a Young Girl*, you might check out from the school library other related books and articles about Greek and Roman mythology, genealogy, history of WWII in Europe, persecution of Jews, concentration camps, tales and legends of the Netherlands, culture and history of the Netherlands, stories of young people who have enriched our world, information about budgeting money/goods, or ways to become a professional writer.

Other things you may keep on hand are puzzles. We have made some relating directly to *Anne Frank: Diary of a Young Girl* for you. Feel free to duplicate them.

Some students may like to draw. You might devise a contest or allow some extra-credit grade for students who draw characters or scenes from *Anne Frank: Diary of a Young Girl*. Note, too, that if the students do not want to keep their drawings you may pick up some extra bulletin board materials this way. If you have a contest and you supply the prize (a CD or something like that perhaps), you could, possibly, make the drawing itself a non-refundable entry fee.

The pages which follow contain games, puzzles and worksheets. The keys, when appropriate, immediately follow the puzzle or worksheet. There are two main groups of activities: one group for the unit; that is, generally relating to the *Anne Frank: Diary of a Young Girl* text, and another group of activities related strictly to the *Anne Frank: Diary of a Young Girl* vocabulary.

Directions for these games, puzzles and worksheets are self-explanatory. The object here is to provide you with extra materials you may use in any way you choose.

MORE ACTIVITIES - *Anne Frank: Diary of a Young Girl*

1. Pick a chapter or scene with a great deal of dialogue and have the students act it out on a stage. (Perhaps you could assign various scenes to different groups of students so more than one scene could be acted and more students could participate.)

2. Have students make a model or a drawing of Anne Frank's annexe.

3. Show the film *Anne Frank: Diary of a Young Girl* after you have completed reading the diary in class. Have students evaluate the movie and compare/contrast it with the book. If the students have tried writing a chapter into a scene in a play, you may wish to discuss how the problems they encountered in changing the form were handled in the movie.

4. Have students design a book cover (front and back and inside flaps) for *Anne Frank: Diary of a Young Girl*.

5. Have students design a bulletin board (ready to be put up; not just sketched) for *Anne Frank: Diary of a Young Girl*.

6. Have students make their own family trees.

7. In her diary, Anne gave the world a portrait of herself, an assessment of her qualities, her hopes, her dreams, her despairs. Have your students write a portrait of themselves.

8. Spend class time discussing productive ways to spend time in a confined area. For example, rainy days at home, travel time in the car, time spent waiting for a ride, etc. Show students what they can accomplish if they use their "wasted" time.

9. See bulletin board idea 9.

10. Do a mini-unit on Judaism. Perhaps compare and contrast it with Christian religions and/or other religions in the world.

11. Anne loved to read. Spend a few days with activities related to the joy/use/importance of reading.

12. Look at WWII from a different angle by reading several short works or excerpts from works written by others involved with WWII. Perhaps have each student read a personal account from different sources and then have the class get back together to discuss the accounts that they read.

WORD SEARCH - *Anne Frank: Diary of a Young Girl*

All words in this list are associated with *Anne Frank: Diary of a Young Girl*. The words are placed backwards, forward, diagonally, up and down. The included words are listed below the word searches.

```
D Q U A R R E L C F P G L C K R P Z F K C Y R O
K N X R J W A W W L S E L H L I T H I P S D T S
Y N A M R E G D M N K M Q H Y O S T S L Z T T V
D I P H T H E R I A K R O B R E T S E W O G A P
D K T X T I I A C O D L M U B Y R H P S F V B R
H S V A L R R T L D L R P T S I L I E S T D E Y
G R E L L T O E L A U I E O A C E K W S P U C Y
D H E C V Y N H N E T S E T T M H E N K T O D W
Q I A P R Z M D S S R X S S S A J I G A P I H Y
H U A N A E N M I C E P S E R M T Q P A R N L R
N R I R D P T T U N U R Z N L E A O T E S F A L
R G D E Y I N P N M A A E D A P T S E P O U W C
F X Q S T E B A J L F K B L W A E T M S T P A S
Q L X T D O T O G R A M R R A G D A E E C F L S
L N G P A N R R I Z N G N R P R C N R L K F D E
F T F R B P U C K O O P H U I S K V A D L K W B
D H D Y W B A F R A N K F O R T K C Q V Y V R Z
```

AFRICA	FRANKFORT	LETTERS	RAID
AMSTERDAM	GERMANY	LIES	RAUTER
ANNEXE	GESTAPO	LOVE	SAUSAGE
BURGLARS	GHANDI	MARGOT	SECRET
CAKE	HENK	MEIP	SHORTHAND
CAMPS	HITLER	MOUSCHI	STAR
CLOTHES	HOLLAND	MUMMY	STILL
CUPBOARD	ITALY	OTTO	STUDY
DENTIST	JEWS	PAPER	TRAINS
DIARY	KISS	PEOPLE	UPSTAIRS
DIPHTHERIA	KITTY	POTATOES	VAN DAANS
DUSSEL	KOLEN	QUARREL	WESTERBORK
ELLI	KOOPHUIS	QUIET	FRANK
KRALER	RADIO		

CROSSWORD - *Anne Frank: Diary of a Young Girl*

CROSSWORD CLUES - *Anne Frank: Diary of a Young Girl*

ACROSS
2. Dussel's occupation
4. They took cashboxes, sugar coupons & more
10. Feeling Anne has for Peter
11. Continent allied forces invaded in 1942
12. Place where Anne & Peter meet in the evenings
14. Things one must have
15. To ingest food
16. Concentration _____
17. Anne saw her pleading, 'Help, oh, help me . . .'
19. Want
21. Meip's husband
23. Hitler wanted to exterminate all of them
24. Depend on
25. The sun's --- came through the window
26. Anne's fictitious diary friend
27. Anne could --- the boys in the street; look at
28. Secret entrance to the annexe
31. One Whom Jews and Christians both worship
34. Henk's wife; office worker; brought news & presents
36. Assumed Mr. Frank's business responsibilities
39. German 'big shot' in Holland; Anne mentions his speech
40. Country to which the Franks moved in 1933
42. Anne's sister
44. Mouschi, for example
46. Verbal fight
49. Mr. Frank
50. Anne loved to read & _____ to pass the time
51. Anne's diary is a --- of her life at the annexe; written document
52. They are the edges of a country
53. Peter's cat

DOWN
1. It 'capitulated' in September 1943
2. Elderly dentist who shares Anne's room
3. Public transportation from which Jews were banned
4. Day Anne's diary starts
5. Freedom-loving, pacifist revolutionary in India
6. Secret _____
7. Mr. Van Daan made meat into this
8. Anne's & Margo's were shabby & too small
9. Country of Anne's birth
11. City where the Secret Annexe was located
13. _____ Annexe
16. Edible Christmas present with 'Peace 1944' written on it
18. She & Meip help keep spirits up in the annexe
20. Stiff; unyielding
21. Leader of Nazi Germany
22. Peter & Anne have a 'goodnight' _____
26. ___ and Co.; firm in which Mr. Frank was a partner
29. It is more patient than man
30. Anne's personal notebook
32. Anne's last name
33. German secret police who came for the Jews
35. 'if ... there weren't any other ___ living in the world.'
37. Mrs. Frank
38. He was especially helpful in arranging logistics & getting food
41. Anne wrote them to Margot and her father
43. Clandestine 'source of courage'
45. Peter, for example
46. Making no sounds
47. Air _____; bombing
48. Yellow ornament Jews had to wear

CROSSWORD ANSWER KEY - *Anne Frank: Diary of a Young Girl*

MATCHING QUIZ/WORKSHEET 1 - *Anne Frank: Diary of a Young Girl*

___ 1. STAR   A. Country to which the Franks moved in 1933

___ 2. MEIP   B. Assumed Mr. Frank's business responsibilities

___ 3. KRALER   C. Air _____; bombing

___ 4. MUMMY   D. Peter & Anne have a 'goodnight' ____

___ 5. BIRTHDAY   E. Anne's personal notebook

___ 6. KISS   F. Secret entrance to the annexe

___ 7. DIPHTHERIA   G. Continent allied forces invaded in 1942

___ 8. GERMANY   H. Country of Anne's birth

___ 9. ITALY   I. Elderly dentist who shares Anne's room

___ 10. POTATOES   J. Concentration _____

___ 11. SECRET   K. Sickness in Elli's home that kept her away for 6 weeks

___ 12. DIARY   L. Mrs. Frank

___ 13. KOLEN   M. It 'capitulated' in September 1943

___ 14. AFRICA   N. ____ Annexe

___ 15. WESTERBORK   O. ___ and Co.; firm in which Mr. Frank was a partner

___ 16. HOLLAND   P. Yellow ornament Jews had to wear

___ 17. DUSSEL   Q. Staple vegetable at the annexe

___ 18. RAID   R. Work camp where many of the Franks' friend were sent

___ 19. CUPBOARD   S. Day Anne's diary starts

___ 20. CAMPS   T. Henk's wife; office worker; brought news & presents

MATCHING QUIZ/WORKSHEET 2 - *Anne Frank: Diary of a Young Girl*

___ 1. RADIO   A. Making no sounds

___ 2. FRANK   B. Dussel's occupation

___ 3. HOLLAND   C. Peter & Anne have a 'goodnight' ____

___ 4. LIES   D. Henk's wife; office worker; brought news & presents

___ 5. SAUSAGE   E. Study of Greek & Roman gods

___ 6. MEIP   F. Feeling Anne has for Peter

___ 7. QUIET   G. Clandestine 'source of courage'

___ 8. LETTERS   H. Anne's last name

___ 9. PEOPLE   I. Work camp where many of the Franks' friends were sent

___ 10. VAN DAANS   J. Public transportation from which Jews were banned

___ 11. WESTERBORK   K. Anne saw her pleading, 'Help, oh, help me . . .'

___ 12. AMSTERDAM   L. Anne wrote them to Margot and her father

___ 13. KISS   M. Country to which the Franks moved in 1933

___ 14. STUDY   N. 'if ... there weren't any other ____ living in the world.'

___ 15. TRAINS   O. City where the Secret Annexe was located

___ 16. MARGOT   P. Anne's & Margo's were shabby & too small

___ 17. LOVE   Q. Family that lived with the Franks in the annexe

___ 18. CLOTHES   R. Mr. Van Daan made meat into this

___ 19. MYTHOLOGY   S. Anne's sister

___ 20. DENTIST   T. Anne loved to read & _____ to pass the time

KEY: MATCHING QUIZ/WORKSHEETS - *Anne Frank: Diary of a Young Girl*

Worksheet 1	Worksheet 2
1. P	1. G
2. T	2. H
3. B	3. M
4. L	4. K
5. S	5. R
6. D	6. D
7. K	7. A
8. H	8. L
9. M	9. N
10. Q	10. Q
11. N	11. I
12. E	12. O
13. O	13. C
14. G	14. T
15. R	15. J
16. A	16. S
17. I	17. F
18. C	18. P
19. F	19. E
20. J	20. B

JUGGLE LETTER REVIEW GAME CLUE SHEET - *Anne Frank: Diary of a Young Girl*

SCRAMBLED	WORD	CLUE
RTFONRKAF	FRANKFORT	City of Anne's birth
RREAUT	RAUTER	German 'big short' in Holland; Anne mentions his speech
DSYTU	STUDY	Anne loved to read
TODNHAHSR	SHORTHAND	Stenographer's written language
RRABSLUG	BURGLARS	They took cashboxes, sugar coupons and more
MPCSA	CAMPS	Concentration _____
TOGRAM	MARGOT	Anne's sister
SSKI	KISS	Peter and Anne have a 'goodnight' _____
OOTT	OTTO	Mr. Frank
SHOUIPOK	KOOPHUIS	He was especially helpful in arranging logistics and getting food
THLOMTGYO	MYTHOLOGY	Study of Greek & Roman Gods
LSTIL	STILL	Making no movements
POPEEL	PEOPLE	'if...there weren't any other _____ living in the world
LERRAK	KRALER	Assumed Mr. Frank's business responsibilities
DBRCPOUA	CUPBOARD	Secret entrance to the annexe
HTIYBARD	BIRTHDAY	Day Anne's diary starts
APERP	PAPER	It is more patient than man
ERREOTKBSW	WESTERBORK	Work camp where many of the Franks friend were sent
CAAFRI	AFRICA	Continent allied forces invaded in 1942
EPMI	MEIP	Henk's wife; office worker; brought news and presents
RSIPSTUA	UPSTAIRS	Place where Anne & Peter meet in the evenings
TREECS	SECRET	_____ Annexe
TLIYA	ITALY	It 'capitulated' in September 1943
ENNAEX	ANNEXE	Secret _____
RYIDA	DIARY	Anne's personal notebook
EKHN	HENK	Meip's husband
LLODHAN	HOLLAND	Country to which the Franks moved in 1933
KECA	CAKE	Edible Christmas present with 'Peace 1944' written on it
ADNSVNAA	VAN DAANS	Family that lived with the Franks in the annexe
TRSA	STAR	Yellow ornament Jews had to wear
SPTOETAO	POTATOES	Staple vegetable at the annexe
TEDAAMSRM	AMSTERDAM	City where the Secret Annexe was located
OIRAD	RADIO	Clandestine 'source of courage'
ETLREST	LETTERS	Anne wrote them to Margot and her father

VOCABULARY RESOURCE MATERIALS

VOCABULARY WORD SEARCH - *Anne Frank: Diary of a Young Girl*

All words in this list are associated with *Anne Frank: Diary of a Young Girl* with an emphasis on the vocabulary words chosen for study in the text. The words are placed backwards, forward, diagonally, up and down. The included words are listed below.

```
J Q C N T L S S W C O N C E I T E D K M R N D H
N D H L U S T A Y A Q B D Q U N A S S U M I N G
B L E N A I I G R P D D E X E L P R E P S O D E
A J C R Y N S L P C M R X L S Z L O H D I T D M
P L T Y U G D A A Y A H O U F V D L A T C U Q L
P R O F I C I E N T T S O I Y A G I A Y R S E C
Y P I O A H O O S C A R M L T N N S L P U T Z K
K G L V F N D R A T E F B M I F N G L O A C X X
C K W I A U A T P T I A Z M U E N D U N K L R K
V A G U E T W T S T T N M L P I B L I S S E H F
T D P S C D I I I M A E M F N F T U N V S D D
W O P I C O O O V C H V O F Q R S O S I I L E R
S H L D T B N E N S F C O L E B U L S T A T L T
Q D S E P U N D B S E C J P O T E S T I A E S F
B U P H R I L X O D S H U S A T E E N R G E W F
J P E Z K A Q A C L M S T F T R U E E N F F R D
C B Q E Y N N U T C E D Q A P Q G B I I B R T X
T N E D R A S T E I V K H P O N I T N L V C Y N
J M Q D X L Q F H D O C O C O L T A Q X P V N J
R E B U K E Y L T Y T N H C W I M M O R T A L K
```

ADO	CONGENIAL	NUISANCE	QUEERLY
ADROIT	COQUETTISH	OBSTINATE	REBUKE
ALOOF	DIN	OPPRESSIVE	SARCASM
ARDENT	DISDAINFUL	PALL	SCOFFINGLY
BLISS	FANATIC	PERPLEXED	SHAMMING
BOISTEROUS	FATALIST	PIQUED	SOLE
CAPITULATION	FATUOUS	PLIED	SUPERFLUOUS
CHATTELS	IMMORTAL	PRIVATIONS	TACT
CLANDESTINE	INEVITABLY	PROCURED	TINGE
COMPENSATION	LIBERATED	PROFICIENT	TOLERANT
CONCEITED	LOATHE	PRUDE	UNASSUMING
CONDOLE	MANIFEST	PSEUDONYM	VAGUE

VOCABULARY CROSSWORD - *Anne Frank: Diary of a Young Girl*

VOCABULARY CROSSWORD CLUES – Anne Frank: Diary of a Young Girl

ACROSS
1. Fervent; passionate
4. Difficult to bear; weighing heavily on the spirit
8. Place where provisions are hidden
11. Bustle; fuss; bother
12. Never to be forgotten
14. Anne's clothes were beginning to look like ---
15. Provoked; full of resentment
16. Edible Christmas present with 'Peace 1944' written on it
17. Word at the end of a prayer
18. Definite article
20. Hitler wanted to exterminate all of them
21. Slight addition
22. Mouschi, for example
23. Henk's wife; office worker; brought news & presents
24. Not on time
25. A thought
26. One who is excessively concerned with being proper
27. Ability to act or speak without offending
29. Sometimes the food at the annexe didn't --- very good
30. Anne saw her pleading, 'Help, oh, help me . . .'
32. Assailed
35. Miss Frank
37. Foolish
39. Pronoun for the Franks
40. Characterized by holding an unusually high opinion of oneself
42. Negative answers
43. Yellow ornament Jews had to wear
44. Extreme happiness
45. Means to; has the intention to
47. Anne's fictitious diary friend
49. Air _____; bombing
50. Mr. Frank
51. Hate; extreme dislike
52. She & Meip help keep spirits up in the annexe
53. Peter & Anne have a 'goodnight' ____
54. Anne's personal notebook

DOWN
1. Reserved; remote
2. Jumble of loud noises
3. Bother
5. Troubled with uncertainty
6. Cutting remarks
7. Not clearly expressed; inexplicit
8. Surrender under specified conditions
9. Characteristic of a woman who makes teasing romantic overtures
10. Improperly forward or bold
11. Skillful and adept under pressure
13. Freed
19. Reprimand; criticize
26. To become dull or boring
28. Personal, movable property
31. Continually, without interruption
33. Despicable; contemptible
34. Loud; lacking in restraint or discipline
36. Friendly
37. Person with an extreme enthusiasm for something
38. Putting on a false appearance
40. To express sympathy
41. That's all; there is no more; the ---
46. Only
48. Meip's husband

VOCABULARY CROSSWORD ANSWER KEY - *Anne Frank: Diary of a Young Girl*

					A	R	D	E	N	T		O	P	P	R	E	S	S	I	V	E
C	A	C	H	E		L		I		U		I		E				A		A	
A		O			A	D	O		N		I	M	M	O	R	T	A	L		R	A	G	S
P	I	Q	U	E	D		O			S		P		P				I		C		U	
I		U		R		F		C	A	K	E			L				B		A	M	E	N
T	H	E		O		R			N		R	E		J	E	W	S						
U		T		T	I	N	G	E		C	A	T		X				R		M	E	I	P
L	A	T	E		T		B			E		I	D	E	A			A					
A		I			P	R	U	D	E			N		D				T	A	C	T		
T	A	S	T	E		A	K		L	I	E	S						E		H		I	
I		H		P	L	I	E	D				N		B			D		A	N	N	E	
O			C		L			I		F	A	T	U	O	U	S			T		C		
N			O					S		A				I		H			T	H	E	M	
	C	O	N	C	E	I	T	E	D		N	O	S		S	T	A	R		E		S	
	O		G		N			A		A			T		M		B	L	I	S	S		
I	N	T	E	N	D	S		K	I	T	T	Y		E			M		S		A		
	D		N		O			N		I			H		R	A	I	D			N		
	O		I		L			F		C	E		O		N			O	T	T	O		
	L	O	A	T	H	E		U			N		U		G					L			
	E		L		E	L	L	I	E		K	I	S	S		D	I	A	R	Y			

VOCABULARY WORKSHEET 1 - *Anne Frank: Diary of a Young Girl*

___ 1. Got by special effort; obtained
    a. Tolerant   b. Prude   c. Procured   d. Shamming

___ 2. To become dull or boring
    a. Piqued   b. Pall   c. Condole   d. Rebuke

___ 3. Freed
    a. Sole   b. Liberated   c. Tinge   d. Proficient

___ 4. Offset; counterbalance; repayment
    a. Tolerant   b. Proficient   c. Tact   d. Compensation

___ 5. Putting on a false appearance
    a. Compensation   b. Shamming   c. Prude   d. Tact

___ 6. Assailed
    a. Plied   b. Pall   c. Ardent   d. Privations

___ 7. Person with an extreme enthusiasm for something
    a. Compensation   b. Perplexed   c. Vague   d. Fanatic

___ 8. Lack of basic necessities of life
    a. Rebuke   b. Unassuming   c. Privations   d. Nuisance

___ 9. One who is excessively concerned with being proper
    a. Fanatic   b. Impertinent   c. Oppressive   d. Prude

___ 10. Adept; expert
    a. Proficient   b. Bliss   c. Ardent   d. Pseudonym

___ 11. Not needed
    a. Aloof   b. Prude   c. Nuisance   d. Superfluous

___ 12. Ability to act or speak without offending
    a. Condole   b. Vague   c. Tact   d. Obstinate

___ 13. Jumble of loud noises
    a. Rebuke   b. Compensation   c. Din   d. Fanatic

___ 14. Despicable; contemptible
    a. Din   b. Immortal   c. Prude   d. Disdainful

___ 15. Bother
    a. Impertinent   b. Plied   c. Nuisance   d. Vague

___ 16. Extreme happiness
    a. Queerly   b. Bliss   c. Oppressive   d. Tolerant

___ 17. Fervent; passionate
    a. Proficient   b. Chattels   c. Pseudonym   d. Ardent

___ 18. Only
    a. Queerly   b. Sole   c. Condole   d. Conceited

___ 19. Difficult to bear; weighing heavily on the spirit
    a. Sarcasm   b. Coquettish   c. Compensation   d. Oppressive

___ 20. Foolish
    a. Congenial   b. Oppressive   c. Fatuous   d. Privations

VOCABULARY WORKSHEET 2 - *Anne Frank: Diary of a Young Girl*

___ 1. TINGE   A. A fictitious name used by an author

___ 2. BLISS   B. Friendly

___ 3. CONCEITED   C. Surrender under specified conditions

___ 4. LOATHE   D. Cutting remarks

___ 5. FATUOUS   E. Ability to act or speak without offending

___ 6. NUISANCE   F. To express sympathy

___ 7. SARCASM   G. Improperly forward or bold

___ 8. CONGENIAL   H. Foolish

___ 9. QUEERLY   I. Extreme happiness

___ 10. OPPRESSIVE   J. Not needed

___ 11. CONDOLE   K. Slight addition

___ 12. INEVITABLY   L. Unavoidably

___ 13. TACT   M. Holding an unusually high opinion of oneself

___ 14. CAPITULATION   N. Difficult to bear; weighing heavily on the spirit

___ 15. SUPERFLUOUS   O. Continually, without interruption

___ 16. PSEUDONYM   P. Reserved; remote

___ 17. IMPERTINENT   Q. Lack of basic necessities of life

___ 18. PRIVATIONS   R. Hate; extreme dislike

___ 19. INCESSANTLY   S. Bother

___ 20. ALOOF   T. Oddly

KEY: VOCABULARY WORKSHEETS - *Anne Frank: Diary of a Young Girl*

Worksheet 1	Worksheet 2
1. C	1. K
2. B	2. I
3. B	3. M
4. D	4. R
5. B	5. H
6. A	6. S
7. D	7. D
8. C	8. B
9. D	9. T
10. A	10. N
11. D	11. F
12. C	12. L
13. C	13. E
14. D	14. C
15. C	15. J
16. B	16. A
17. D	17. G
18. B	18. Q
19. D	19. O
20. C	20. P

VOCABULARY REVIEW GAME CLUES - *Anne Frank: Diary of a Young Girl*

SCRAMBLED	WORD	CLUE
ROIATD	ADROIT	Skillful and adept under pressure
IANCESNU	NUISANCE	Bother
BLTADRIEE	LIBERATED	Freed
VSEPPEIRSO	OPPRESSIVE	Difficult to bear; weighing heavily on the spirit
LESO	SOLE	Only
OTNRETLA	TOLERANT	Inclined to put up with beliefs, practices or traits of others
IDEPUQ	PIQUED	Provoked; full of resentment
DETNAR	ARDENT	Fervent; passionate
LYQREEU	QUEERLY	Oddly
ENCIDECOT	CONCEITED	Holding an unusually high opinion of oneself
TPEITREMNNI	IMPERTINENT	Improperly forward or bold
DEPIL	PLIED	Assailed
SSLBI	BLISS	Extreme happiness
YNDSEMOPU	PSEUDONYM	A fictitious name used by an author
ACMASSR	SARCASM	Cutting remarks
IND	DIN	Jumble of loud noises
GTEIN	TINGE	Slight addition
AVUEG	VAGUE	Not clearly expressed; inexplicit
OUSISREOTB	BOISTEROUS	Loud; lacking in restraint or discipline
TDNSLCEEAIN	CLANDESTINE	Kept secret to conceal an improper purpose
TTAC	TACT	Ability to act or speak without offending
MNSHIGMA	SHAMMING	Putting on a false appearance
TCSYINLAENS	INCESSANTLY	Continually, without interruption
UFSTUOA	FATUOUS	Foolish
EOTSTBNIA	OBSTINATE	Stubborn
RUPRDCOE	PROCURED	Got by special effort; obtained
UEEBRK	REBUKE	Reprimand; criticize
LPAL	PALL	To become dull or boring
EDRPU	PRUDE	One who is excessively concerned with being proper
USIILDFNDA	DISDAINFUL	Despicable; contemptible
IAVITNORSP	PRIVATIONS	Lack of basic necessities of life
RPEEPLEDX	PERPLEXED	Troubled with uncertainty
OLOCNED	CONDOLE	To express sympathy
EATHLO	LOATHE	Hate; extreme dislike
RUFOSPULSUE	SUPERFLUOUS	Not needed
SACINUEN	NUISANCE	Bother